THE GREEN BELT
MOVEMENT

THE GREEN BELT MOVEMENT

MOVEMENT

*Sharing the Approach
and the Experience*

WANGARI MAATHAI

LANTERN BOOKS • NEW YORK

A DIVISION OF BOOKLIGHT INC.

2004
Lantern Books
One Union Square West, Suite 201
New York, NY 10003

Copyright Wangari Maathai 2003, 2004

First edition published in 1985, revised 2003, 2004

Design and Separations by: Eyes on Africa, P.O. Box 67477, Nairobi, Kenya.
Cover photograph: Mia MacDonald

Interview with Wangari Maathai: Source: *World Watch*, Vol. 17, No. 3, copyright 2004, www.worldwatch.org

Printed in the United States of America

Library of Congress Cataloging-in-Publication Data

Maathai, Wangari.
The Green Belt Movement : sharing the approach and the experience / Wangari Maathai.—Rev. ed.
p. cm.
ISBN 1-59056-040-X (alk. paper)
1. Green Belt Movement (Society : Kenya) 2. Tree planting—Kenya. I. Green Belt Movement (Society : Kenya) II. Title.
SB435.6.K4M33 2003
333.75'153'096762—dc21
2002012116

NEW LEAF PAPER

ENVIRONMENTAL BENEFITS STATEMENT

The Green Belt Movement is printed on New Leaf EcoBook 100, made with 100% post-con-sumer waste, processed chlorine free. By using this environmentally friendly paper, Lantern Books saved the following resources:

trees	water	energy	solid waste	greenhouse gases
40 fully grown	**17,063** gallons	**29** million BTUs	**1,903** pounds	**3,750** pounds

Calculated based on research done by Environmental Defense and other members of the Paper Task Force.

© New Leaf Paper   Visit us in cyberspace at www.newleafpaper.com or call 1-888-989-5323

TABLE OF CONTENTS

ACKNOWLEDGMENTS

The responsibility and privilege of writing about the Green Belt Movement has fallen upon me. However, the material on these pages is the product of the dedication of thousands of Green Belt members, associates, volunteers and donors. Without them, there would be no Green Belt Movement to write about.

It is impossible to mention by name all those who light the path of an author, and I have had many along my path: friends, colleagues, coworkers and members of my extended family. The debt can never be paid.

The first edition of this book was written with the assistance of the Environment Liaison Center International (ELCI). For this second edition, the manuscript would still be collecting dust on the shelf were it not for the devoted effort of Muta, who knew I was eager to share the story but lacked the time to complete it. He worked hard at it, sometimes into the night, and I am very grateful for his help, encouragement and commitment.

Lantern Books, through the intervention of Martin Rowe, met the cost of printing this book, along with the Government of Austria through CARE Austria. For this support and indeed for supporting other programs of the Green Belt Movement for many years, we are deeply indebted.

Sometimes I have come across articles, books and statements that say exactly what I wish to say but in a much better way. I am grateful to all those sources of inspiration.

Wangari Maathai

2004 NOBEL PEACE PRIZE
ANNOUNCEMENT

The Norwegian Nobel Committee has decided to award the Nobel Peace Prize for 2004 to Wangari Maathai for her contribution to sustainable development, democracy and peace.

Peace on earth depends on our ability to secure our living environment. Maathai stands at the front of the fight to promote ecologically viable social, economic and cultural development in Kenya and in Africa. She has taken a holistic approach to sustainable development that embraces democracy, human rights and women's rights in particular. She thinks globally and acts locally.

Maathai stood up courageously against the former oppressive regime in Kenya. Her unique forms of action have contributed to drawing attention to political oppression—nationally and internationally. She has served as inspiration for many in the fight for democratic rights and has especially encouraged women to better their situation.

Maathai combines science, social commitment and active politics. More than simply protecting the existing environment, her strategy is to secure and strengthen the very basis for ecologically sustainable development. She founded the Green Belt

Movement where, for nearly 30 years, she has mobilized poor women to plant 30 million trees. Her methods have been adopted by other countries as well. We are all witness to how deforestation and forest loss have led to desertification in Africa and threatened many other regions of the world—in Europe too. Protecting forests against desertification is a vital factor in the struggle to strengthen the living environment of our common Earth.

Through education, family planning, nutrition and the fight against corruption, the Green Belt Movement has paved the way for development at the grassroots level. We believe that Maathai is a strong voice speaking for the best forces in Africa to promote peace and good living conditions on that continent.

Wangari Maathai will be the first woman from Africa to be honored with the Nobel Peace Prize. She will also be the first African from the vast area between South Africa and Egypt to be awarded the prize. She represents an example and a source of inspiration for everyone in Africa fighting for sustainable development, democracy and peace.

STATEMENT FROM
WANGARI MAATHAI

I would like to thank the Nobel Committee for the unparalleled honor of being awarded the Nobel Peace Prize for 2004. By making this award, the Nobel Committee has placed the critical issues of environmental conservation, democratic governance, community empowerment and peace before the eyes of the world, and for that I am profoundly grateful. The 30 million trees planted by Green Belt Movement volunteers—mostly rural women—throughout Kenya over the past 30 years are a testament to individuals' ability to change the course of environmental history.

Working together, we have proven that sustainable development is possible; that reforestation of degraded land is possible; and that exemplary governance is possible when ordinary citizens are informed, sensitized, mobilized and involved in direct action for their environment.

This is a great day for Kenya and especially for members of the Green Belt Movement and the global green movement. It is also a wonderful opportunity to help inspire the nations of the world toward the goals of environmental sustainability, human rights, gender equality and peace. On behalf of all African women, I want to express my profound appreciation for this honor, which will serve to encourage women in Kenya, in Africa and around the world to raise their voices and not to be deterred.

I also want to thank the press here in Kenya and around the world for walking with us in bad and good times.

After 30 years of struggle to renew Kenya's natural resources and instill a sense of responsibility and ownership at the grass-roots level, this elevation to the august company of Nobel laureates like Nelson Mandela, Desmond Tutu, Kofi Annan, Martin Luther King, Jr. and Shireen Ebadi is a totally unexpected and gratifying validation.

Some people have asked what the relationship is between peace and environment, and to them I say that many wars are fought over resources, which are becoming increasingly scarce across the earth. If we did a better job of managing our resources sustainably, conflicts over them would be reduced. So, protecting the global environment is directly related to securing peace.

Many people have asked me through the years of struggle how I have kept going, how I have continued even when my ideas and my work were challenged or even ignored. Those of us who understand the complex concept of the environment have the burden to act. We must not tire, we must not give up, we must persist.

I would like to call on young people, in particular, to take inspiration from this prize. Despite all the constraints that they face, there is hope in the future in serving the common good. What my experiences have taught me is that service to others has its own special rewards.

When we plant trees, we plant the seeds of peace and seeds of hope. We also secure the future for our children. One of the first things I did yesterday when I got the extraordinary news about this prize was to plant a Nandi flame tree. It was at the foot of Mt. Kenya, which has been a source of inspiration to me and to generations before me.

So, on this wonderful occasion, I call on all Kenyans and those around the world to celebrate by planting a tree wherever you are. Once again, I want to thank members of the press, members of the Green Belt Movement, friends who have been with me all along, and my three children, Waweru, Wanjira and Muta.

Thank you.

PREFACE

A lot has happened to me since this book was completed in July 2002. For one, I ran for Parliament later in the year in Kenya's first democratic elections in nearly a quarter-century, and was elected to represent Tetu constituency in Nyeri district of Central Kenya. That is the region where I was born and spent most of my childhood. Nyeri sits at the foot of Mount Kenya, the second highest mountain in Africa, which was sacred not only to my Kikuyu community, but also to other communities living around it. The mountain continues to be a source of inspiration to me, especially with respect to cultural biodiversity.

In 2003, Kenya's President, Mwai Kibaki, appointed me assistant minister for environment and natural resources. In this post I have been focusing on the restoration of forests and other environmental issues. I have also been representing Tetu constituency in Parliament.

On weekends, I visit Tetu to work with the constituents on development projects. On October 8th 2004, I was on my way there when I received news that I still find quite overwhelming: The Nobel Peace Committee had named me the winner of the 2004 Nobel Peace Prize. I could hardly believe it. My heart filled with emotion, bringing tears to my eyes as I faced my favorite mountain, Mt. Kenya. The news also brought Kenya, especially women, a lot of energy, hope and a sense of gratification. Many women in Africa and indeed the world felt a deep sense of satisfaction as they reflected on their work to protect the environment, promote democratic governance and build respect for human rights and peace.

The Prize has brought with it new energy but also new responsibilities, especially during the year of the Prize. The Prize is a strong recognition for the work of so many women, men and children at the grassroots level. It is there that the Green Belt Movement, which is the focus of this book, puts its energy.

The Green Belt Movement has over the past 30 years shown that sustainable development linked with democratic values promotes human rights, social justice and equity, including the balance of power between women and men. The Prize demonstrates that although the work of grassroots groups, especially women's groups, does not always make headline news, it does make a difference.

Women around the world first came together in 1975 in Mexico City, under the auspices of the United Nations. Since then, women have been demanding to be heard and counted, to be put at the center stage of decision-making. Sometimes they find themselves there; at other times they find themselves at the edge of the stage or off the stage altogether. Now that the Nobel Committee has put women among the stars, it is very important for them to strive to stay there and not come down.

The Nobel award supports my strong view that wherever they live and whatever role or position they hold in society, all people appreciate the connection between good environmental management, good democratic governance and peace. Honestly, as I write this, I am still pinching myself and telling myself that it is not a dream. I know that the Nobel Committee awards the

Prize to an individual or to organizations. But the 2004 Nobel Peace Prize was directed at a large constituency of women, environmentalists, promoters of democratic governance and peace advocates everywhere. This is a huge global constituency, and I call upon its members to celebrate this recognition, use it to advance their mission and live up to the expectations created by this award.

When people ask me how I managed to keep going even when the work of the Green Belt Movement was ignored or ridiculed, or the ideas and the people working with the movement were physically attacked, often viciously, my response is that if we do not project fear, we are able to progress despite the odds and step by step we can reach our destination. I hope that all those who feel touched and encouraged by this work and the Peace Prize will continue taking the right steps for the environment, for democracy and for peace—whether this work is in the developing or in the developed world.

It has been a long walk to the Peace Prize. I want to thank those who have walked with me, both physically and in spirit. I do not see the Prize as a destination, but rather as an extraordinary opportunity that has been given not just to me but to all people in the world who share the values and vision that the Peace Prize Committee recognized.

As I said in my statement earlier in this book, I would urge all those who wish to celebrate the Prize to plant a tree. In the meantime, enjoy this book, learn from it, take the lessons with you and share them.

Wangari Maathai
NAIROBI, OCTOBER 2004

FOREWORD

I t is a great pleasure for me to contribute to this book on the Green Belt Movement of Kenya by Wangari Maathai. The Green Belt Movement has obtained a very important position, in particular among those of us who are strongly committed to the issues of the environment and development. It represents an example of how grassroots initiatives can lead to change. The Movement has increased the awareness of citizens and decision-makers alike. In particular, the efforts of women and young people all over Kenya have helped to make the Movement a success.

In the words of Wangari Maathai, the healing of Africans is still a dream. However, the dream may someday become a reality. After all, trees are a symbol of hope. Encouraging developments in some parts of Africa may indicate that a new greening is possible. Local initiatives have yielded concrete results, and many governments are addressing the problems of deforestation in a more responsible manner—often in cooperation with Non-Governmental Organizations (NGOs) and grassroots movements.

The World Commission on Environment and Development called for increasing influence and greater resources to be accorded to initiatives such as the Green Belt Movement. I believe that concrete results achieved by the Green Belt Movement will continue to serve as a source of inspiration whose significance will extend far beyond the borders of Kenya. And this book is an important means by which this inspiration will become widely disseminated.

Dr. Gro Harlem Brundtland,
Former Prime Minister of Norway and Former Chair of the World
Commission on Environment and Development

1: INTRODUCTION

As we entered the twenty-first century, the Green Belt Movement (GBM) was experiencing a rebirth through a new strategic plan. Because this plan significantly reorganized GBM, it was perceived as a milestone. Thus, in order to differentiate the activities of the organization prior to the strategic plan from those that were to follow that planning process, the terms Phase I and Phase II, respectively, were introduced.

This book is a record of the Phase I experience. It mainly focuses on the activities of GBM from its beginning up to 1999—the year that the strategic planning commenced. However, to give readers some insight into what lies ahead for the organization, elements of the Phase II plan will be mentioned.

The Green Belt Movement has been functional in Kenya for well over two decades now, and therefore to clearly understand its operations one needs to have some knowledge of the country. A lot of information has already been published on Kenya and need not be repeated here. However, a brief introduction will suffice to highlight the information that is relevant to understanding GBM.

Kenya is located on the eastern coast of Africa and has a size

Fig 1.1: An indigenous forest in Kenya

of 582,644 km². The capital city is Nairobi. The equator runs across the country and divides it into two nearly equal parts.

Kenya's relief is varied, with altitudes ranging from sea-level to slightly above 5,000 meters. Its relief features include plateaus, plains, highlands, the lake basin and the Rift Valley. The natural vegetation in the country falls into four main categories: heath and moorland, savanna grassland, scrub and semi-desert, and forest (see fig. 1.1). Currently, the total forested area in Kenya is less than two percent; scrub and semi-desert covers the largest area, followed by savanna grassland.

The country has a population of approximately 30 million people, with each belonging to one of the 42 communities; although there are many similarities between those communities, each has its unique culture. These communities include the Luo,

Kikuyu, Kamba, Luhya, Maasai, Meru, Embu, Somali and Turkana.

To the North, Kenya is bordered by Sudan and Ethiopia, to the West by Uganda and Lake Victoria, to the South by Tanzania and to the East by Somalia and the Indian Ocean. These borders were drawn during the colonial rule that Kenya, and most other African countries, underwent from the late nineteenth century up to the early 1960s. Kenya was colonized and ruled by the British until 1963 when it got independence after an armed struggle known as the Mau Mau Movement.

The system of governance that the British introduced during the colonial period is in many ways still used today in various sectors. For instance, the British colonialists divided Kenya into regions so as to better control the indigenous people. After independence, the new local government decided to maintain these regions (or administrative units), and it is through these units that the people of Kenya continue to be governed.

The largest of these administrative units are the provinces, which are governed by Provincial Commissioners (PC). The provinces are eight in number as listed below.

CENTRAL	NORTHERN-EASTERN
COAST	NYANZA
EASTERN	RIFT VALLEY
NAIROBI	WESTERN

The capital city constitutes Nairobi province. Provinces are in turn divided into districts, districts into divisions, divisions into locations, and locations into sub-locations; a sub-location is therefore the smallest administrative unit. A district is governed by a District Commissioner (DC), a division by a Divisional Officer (DO), a location by a Chief, and a sub-location by a Sub-chief. As of March 1999, there were 68 districts, 483 divisions, 2,354 locations and 6,431 sub-locations.

When drawing the boundaries for the administrative units, the British colonialists did not consult with the indigenous people. In some areas the boundaries cut right through communities so that today, people residing in neighboring provinces are likely to belong to different communities. The Green Belt Movement recognizes this problem but nevertheless uses the current administrative system in its work since infrastructure and important development services (e.g. government extension workers) base their work upon it.

Kenya is also divided into constituencies. A constituency is the area that an elected Member of Parliament (MP) represents. Currently there are 210 constituencies, many of which have boundaries similar to those of divisions. In some cases however, constituencies consist of more than one division.

From the mid-sixties until 1992, all MPs had to belong to the one political party, the Kenya African National Union (KANU). In late 1991, however, the movement for multipartism reached its climax with a constitutional change that re-introduced a multi-party political system. From it, two major political factions emerged: the ruling party, and all the other new political parties, which form what is now commonly referred to as the Opposition.

Depending on the level of development attained, the country is divided into rural and urban areas. At present, a large majority of Kenyans reside in rural areas, which still require much development if the quality of life in those communities is to be enhanced.

In Kenya, rural development is conducted in several ways. But one very common way is through the formation of government-registered development groups. Members of such groups usually reside in the same sub-location and have some commonality (e.g. they have similar occupations, worship in the same church, etc.). There are various reasons why people form groups. These include the desire to raise capital for self-help projects and socialization, or to strengthen ties between family and/or friends. It is important to note that a large majority of the members in such groups are women; this explains why development groups are also commonly referred to as women's groups.

2: THE HISTORY OF THE GREEN BELT MOVEMENT

The Green Belt Movement is a grassroots Non-Governmental Organization (NGO) that focuses on environment conservation and development. It does this mainly through a nationwide grassroots tree-planting campaign that is its core activity. Unlike many other organizations in Africa, it is not a branch of a foreign NGO but an indigenous initiative, registered and headquartered in Nairobi. It is wholly managed by Kenyans and deliberately prefers to rely on local capacity, knowledge, wisdom and expertise where appropriate. Although it has members in both urban and rural areas, most members are in the rural areas, and a very large majority of them are women.

The Green Belt Movement, in its current structure and mode of operation, is the result of a vision that has undergone great transformation over time through the efforts of many diligent and committed people who have generously given themselves to the service of the organization (*see fig. 2.1*). GBM has also been shaped by its partners and friends, who have contributed significantly to its development. It has indeed been a long but enriching walk for many.

As early as the 1920s, several years before the dawn of the modern environmental movement, enthusiasts like the late Ex-

Fig. 2.1: Austrian Ambassador H.E. Franz Hoerlberger (seated center) at GBM's Lang'ata training center with Board members standing from left: Jane Ngugi, Miriam Chege, Canute Khamala, Ngere Rubia, Lilian Wanjiru Njehu and Lilian Mwaura. Seated from left are Vertistine B. Mbaya and Wangari Maathai.

Fig 2.2: Ex-Senior Chief Josiah Njonjo (second right in dark suit) leading a tree-planting event at Naivasha in 1978. With him is the author (with white head band), members of Men of the Trees and members of the local community.

Senior Chief Josiah Njonjo and Dr. St. Barb Baker had introduced a participatory community reforestation program through
an organization known as Men of the Trees (*see fig. 2.2*). After
Njonjo's death, the organization became inactive in Kenya,
though it remained vibrant in Britain. There were also other environmental enthusiasts who were raising awareness and warning
the world about issues such as acid rain, loss of wilderness and
threats to various biological resources.

In 1972, the environmental movement took a major step forward: the United Nations Environment Programme (UNEP) was
established in Nairobi as a result of the United Nations Conference on Human Environment held in Stockholm in the same
year. This development helped arouse interest in the environment
in Africa despite the fact that many governments in the region
were not in favor of the policies adopted in Stockholm to curb
environmental degradation. They argued that the Northern industrialized countries were hindering the industrialization and development of Africa by introducing anti-development policies and
conditions.

The establishment of UNEP in Nairobi attracted a few
Northern NGOs that wanted to establish close working ties with
UNEP as well as ensure that the agreements made in Stockholm
were implemented. To achieve this, the NGOs established a
center called the Environment Liaison Center (ELC) and
elected themselves as the first board members. Since they
resided in the North, however, they decided to involve local persons who could become alternate board members and supervise
the day-to-day running of the organization. At the time, I was
serving as the Director of Kenya Red Cross-Nairobi Branch, and,
with the invitation of Oscar Mann, I accepted an invitation to
join the ELC board as an alternate for Huey Johnson of the

Resource Renewal Institute in California, USA. It was enriching to be involved in the Environment Liaison Center, which grew by leaps and bounds.

After some years, my colleagues elected me Chairman of the Board. I became a good student of the environment and developed a strong affiliation with it. My background as a biological scientist and daughter of a peasant farmer provided the seed for growth and long-term commitment to the environment. I was slowly becoming a strong environmental advocate. Fortunately for us alternate board members, both the Director of UNEP at the time, Maurice Strong, and his deputy, Mustafa Tolba (who later became its Executive Director), were great supporters of ELC, and so we received a lot of encouragement and learned a great deal from them about the environment. They became lifetime friends and have continued to support our work—though they are no longer heading UNEP. At ELC, we continued to monitor the relationship between NGOs and UNEP and were all pleased with the progress. Indeed, it is this relationship that played a role in the acceptance of many local and small NGOs into the UN system and also provided opportunities for cooperation between NGOs and UN programs. After several years, ELC changed its name to Environment Liaison Center International (ELCI), which it still uses today.

It was not until 1974 that I began to focus on issues of forestation and reforestation. During that time I was involved in a political campaign to elect Mwangi, my husband at the time and father of our three children, as a Member of Parliament for Lang'ata, a constituency in Nairobi province (*see fig. 2.3*). In our campaign meetings and rallies we discussed many of the constituents' concerns, the most frequent being lack of employment for them and their own children, and assured them of our com-

Fig 2.3: *The author (left) on a campaign trail with women led by Nyina wa Kangi (right) in 1973.*

mitment to provide adequate solutions. Perhaps because I was naive, I took the political promises that we made to the voters seriously and agonized over finding ways to have them fulfilled, especially if we won the elections. Now, many years down the road and with a lot of experience, I realize that the approach that I had, and still have, toward public service is one shared by a minority of people. I assumed that all people working in public service loved the people they served, were accountable and transparent, and had integrity. That was part of the culture that had been inculcated in me by my parents and teachers. It was part of my personality, character and conscience. I have since learned that such assumptions are shared by few.

By introducing and pursuing a tree-planting activity to provide the jobs we had promised during the campaign, I was following my conscience and doing the right thing. Anything to the contrary would have made our campaign a sham. Unfortunately, I had not understood that most politicians necessarily ran their campaigns by taking advantage of voters, especially because the voters also tried hard to take advantage of politicians—more so financially. This is the game that majority of politicians play with their constituents, and vice versa. Sadly, the game continues even today.

Fortunately, we won the elections. My husband was very happy and went on to Parliament. I attended his swearing-in and was truly proud of him as he took the oath of office. Having accomplished that, I returned to the constituents to try to meet some of the promises we had made to them. I was then alone except for Mr. Murefu, a family friend who had campaigned alongside me for Mwangi. He believed in me.

During the campaign period, Murefu had introduced me to Mr. Kimathi, a forester who was in charge of Karura forest. We told Kimathi of our intention to establish a tree nursery to enable us employ Lang'ata constituents to plant trees in the non-forested areas of the city. He was very supportive and therefore allowed us to establish a tree nursery at the forest (just next to the forest tree nursery), and gave us all the seedlings and the technical advice that we needed. We hired a young man called Charles Githogori to manage that small project and collect containers into which seedlings could be transplanted. This became the first tree nursery, and it gave us the confidence that our promise to the Lang'ata constituents would materialize. Shortly after that, I formed Envirocare Ltd., a company that was going to hire constituents to clean up the homesteads of residents in Lang'ata as well as plant trees where necessary. Envirocare, which was headquartered in our home, was also supposed to provide a forum for our interaction with the Lang'ata constituents.

The establishment of the company was inspired by the sheer enthusiasm of a young and idealistic Kikuyu woman, from the beautiful hills of Nyeri, whose life had been enriched by rewarding experiences, especially while in the United States of America and West Germany. After completing my studies in the U.S., I was fully energized and indeed ready and eager to play a role in the development of Kenya. When in later years I became vilified and the Green Belt Movement became trivialized as a Kikuyu organization, I would go back to these humble origins and reconfirm to myself the fact that what I had began doing in my early thirties was inspired by and for the common good. I had no idea what would become of it but had what it took: inspiration, persistence, patience and commitment.

My concerns, energies and successes had nothing to do with my womanhood, marital status or community of affiliation. It was truly coincidental that I was a woman and a Kikuyu from

Nyeri. For that reason, when I would later be dismissed on account of my tribe and marital status, I knew that much of the malice was due to jealousy and political expediency.

Envirocare received a positive response from only a few constituents. This was because those hired were poor and needed payment even before work was completed! They expected me to facilitate them in every way, including transporting them to work. Unfortunately, I had to learn the hard way that poor people can make themselves too much of a burden for one to assist them. Because of such difficulties, the company did not take off as expected. Despite this, I persisted and begun to look into ways to further promote Envirocare to potential clients. The International Show seemed like the right forum for this.

Since Kenya is primarily an agricultural country, the government uses various forums to promote this and other economic sectors, both locally and internationally. One such forum is the International Show, an annual event held in various parts of the country to achieve a variety of aims, including the creation of a forum where public awareness on agricultural and other issues can be raised. A few weeks before the 1975 International Show in Nairobi, it was decided that Envirocare would participate, because we envisioned the event as an ideal place to publicize the company and its tree-planting activity further. We quickly acquired a stand, transferred all our seedlings there from Karura forest and arranged them so as to depict a map of Kenya, highlighting the many areas that required intensive tree planting.

During the five-day long show, people visited our stand with interest, and some even requested our physical address. Unfortunately, as we had not found an ideal site for the seedlings by that time, only a mailing address was distributed. Despite this, the show gave us an opportunity to gauge people's interest in tree planting. We concluded that a lot of people wanted to plant trees, based on the interesting conversations we engaged in regarding tree species and their utility and availability. We also observed that people wanted to obtain seedlings cheaply, and that they wanted to plant them on their up-country farms and not in Nairobi. This confirmed to us that many people expected the City Council, and not themselves, to plant trees in urban centers. This observation proved helpful, especially when the tree-planting activity was taken to the rural areas.

After the show, we shifted the seedlings to the backyard of our home at Kabarnet Road instead of returning them to Karura forest and continued to look for appropriate office space.

Envirocare never generated the financial resources needed to operate optimally because the income gained from the few people that it employed was minimal. Further, and to our dismay, none of those to whom we gave our address at the Show corresponded or came to collect seedlings. Although this was disappointing, we kept Envirocare functional. Meanwhile, additional difficulties arose in the form of little help from those close to me. Without support and with such a poor constituency to work with, Envirocare came to a halt and became dormant.

In our attempt to fully establish and implement the vision of Envirocare, there were some discouraging moments, but there were also some very encouraging times. One such rejuvenating period occurred in June 1976, when the United Nations held a conference on Human Settlements (HABITAT I) in Vancouver, Canada. I attended the conference through the assistance of some staff members from the United Nations Environment Program in Kenya, especially Hanna Mastrand Strong. Hanna and I had become friends through our work for street children at the Kenya Red Cross Society.

While in Vancouver I met people who, like myself, were eager to work for improved societal living conditions. I had an opportunity to meet, address and listen to many of the speakers, and was particularly impressed by Margaret Mead, Mother Teresa and Barbara Ward, all of whom were also friends of Hanna. I also had time to reflect on all the issues that we at the conference were being bombarded with. These included the need to appreciate that planet earth is our only "ship" and therefore needed ethical steering, a halt to over-exploitation of resources, the need to control the development of cities to prevent the creation of "concrete jungles," and the problem of air pollution through road transport. People everywhere were calling for better cities—especially for more trees and green vegetation. I was particularly pleased with the call for citizens to take action to improve human settlements.

I returned to Kenya after a wonderful two weeks of encouragement in beautiful Vancouver, with renewed commitment and energy, determined to make Envirocare more effective. I set out to work on the tree nursery, which was now sprawling around the entire compound. The sight was not attractive, and my husband did not think the idea was viable. Furthermore, there was a shortage of water in Nairobi that resulted in the release of a government order that forbade all Nairobi residents to use water for secondary purposes, such as watering flower gardens. With neither support from the household nor a readily available water supply, most of the seedlings died and the tree nursery collapsed.

Without alternative space for my creative spirit, the Envirocare initiative would have ceased. However, the idea of planting trees with the people found another forum through the National Council of Women of Kenya (NCWK). In the midst of frustrated energies, I received an invitation from the Chairman of the

National Council of Women of Kenya, then nominated Member of Parliament Hon. Eddah Gachukia, to attend their Annual General Meeting and give a lecture on my experiences at HABITAT I. This was in 1977.

I was honored to be invited and glad that my presentation was well received. When responding to the audience's enthusiastic questions and comments, I would not have guessed that our interaction would provide a new opportunity for both Envirocare and myself. Some months later, I received a letter from the Chairman stating that I had been elected a member of the Executive Committee of NCWK and of the Standing Committee on Environment and Habitat.

As a member of the National Association of University Women, I was eligible for election, but to have been selected after only a short period of interaction with the members was certainly a demonstration of much confidence. I felt a deep sense of commitment to them that greatly influenced my future work in NCWK. This was especially because I had not had much experience in women's organizations per se. I was a member of an elite women's group pursuing excellence in the academic field and was therefore uncertain of what my contribution to NCWK would be, especially because the majority of its members were, and still are, rural women. Nevertheless, in the spirit that I now recognize as part of my personality, I fully embraced the opportunity this challenge provided. With time, it indeed proved to be a wonderful forum with meaningful experiences though quite far removed from the ivory tower of a university classroom.

The NCWK is an organization that provides a common forum of action for scores of national women's organizations and groups, both rural and urban. It was conceived and founded in 1964, one year after Kenya attained independence. Its constitution and objectives were fashioned in a manner similar to that of the International Council of Women, which was founded in the U.S.A in 1888. After its registration in Kenya in 1966, NCWK became affiliated with the International Council of Women in the same year. Its mode of operation was through an Executive Committee; each Executive Committee member was also a member of a standing committee.

When I joined the Standing Committee on Environment and Habitat, I participated in discussions on various issues, including the identification of potential conservation activities that the organization could engage in. The idea of tree planting was still very much alive in me, and so were the inspirations I had gained at the HABITAT I conference in Vancouver. However, I did not see the standing committee as an opportunity to revive Envirocare and the tree-planting initiative. That came almost by accident, and this is how it happened.

As a standing committee member, I worked closely with the chairwoman, Wanjiku Chiuri, and the secretary, Rhoda Thairu. Occasionally, both would find themselves extremely occupied and would therefore request me to chair the committee meetings for them. This responsibility required that I provide direction and facilitate discussions during the meeting. It was during one such gathering that I highlighted tree planting as a potential activity for NCWK. I proposed it as a project that would especially help our members in the rural areas to inexpensively meet many of their needs including wood fuel, building and fencing material and soil conservation. Indeed, I had earlier attended a seminar organized by the NCWK that highlighted—with astonishing data—the problem of malnutrition, especially among children and the elderly, in Central province. It showed that malnutrition was a problem affecting both the poor and the affluent alike. The regions covered in the study included Nyeri, the district where I grew up without ever hearing of malnutrition.

The speaker touched on three factors that, according to her study, were the causes of the observed health problem. Her first point was that farmers had increased cash-crop farming at the expense of subsistence farming with the rationale that a given area of land under cash-crop farming could generate an income large enough to purchase enough food for the household, meet other expenses like school fees and clothing and still leave some finances for investment (see fig. 2.4). Unfortunately, because of severe mismanagement in government parastatals, cooperatives and the local management committees, some farmers went unpaid while those who received some income were underpaid, at irregular intervals! This left them without sufficient finances to provide balanced diets for their families, and that led to malnutrition. In recent years the mismanagement of cash crops has led to violent clashes between the administration and the farmers.

Secondly, farmers with moderate incomes tended to ignore the traditional unprocessed foods such as sweet potatoes, yams and cassava, as well as indigenous green vegetables. Instead, they changed their diets so as to match those of the affluent, many of who were living in the urban areas. However, because of the high costs of such foods, some farmers were unable to regularly provide them for their families. Therefore, they ended up with diets rich in certain nutrients (especially carbohydrates) but poor in others, like proteins and vitamins. This left families malnourished.

The speaker's third point was linked to the fact that about 90 percent of the people living in the rural areas use wood fuel for cooking and heating their houses. With the demand higher than the supply, she observed that the scarcity of wood fuel forced

Fig 2.4: *The author (foreground) demonstrates to some visitors the art of picking coffee berries.*

some families to eat food that mainly required relatively little fuel to cook, regardless of its nutritional value. This also led to malnutrition.

Each problem required a unique solution. Tree planting at the community level seemed like an appropriate way to increase the supply of wood fuel even in the long term; however, the standing committee thought otherwise. They argued that such a project could only be carried out by foresters and did not fit into the goals of NCWK, and could therefore not be carried out by people at the grass roots since they lacked the expertise required to manage tree nurseries. Even so, it was the only idea that was forthcoming at the time and was therefore accepted as a project of the Environment and Habitat committee and NCWK. That acceptance, which occurred in 1977, was a milestone for Envirocare because it had now been transferred from my personal and family domain to that of an organization. I did not persuade the members of the committee to adopt the name Envirocare but instead came up with another name that better explained the objective of the project: to carry out a tree-planting campaign through the *Harambee* spirit.

Harambee means "Let us all pull together!" Many communities used and still use the word "harambee" to boost the morale of participants during communal work. The word was popularized and made into a national slogan by the late Mzee Jomo Kenyatta, the first president of Kenya. In his early political rallies, he galvanized Kenyans around this slogan and called upon them to unite for the advancement of their new nation. I suggested that we call the NCWK campaign "Save the Land Harambee." Rather than collect funds for community projects, Kenyans would be encouraged to collectively re-dedicate themselves to save their country from the threat of desertification through their active participation in forestation and reforestation. At every tree-planting ceremony, the participants re-affirmed their dedication to this cause by reciting the following committal:

> Being aware that Kenya is being threatened by the expansion of desert-like conditions; that desertification comes as a result of misuse of the land and by consequent soil erosion by the elements; and that these actions result in drought, malnutrition, famine and death; we resolve to save our land by averting this same desertification through the planting of trees wherever possible. In pronouncing these words, we each make a personal commitment to save our country from actions and elements which would deprive present and future generations from reaping the bounty [of resources] which is the birthright and property of all.

The first Save the Land Harambee tree-planting ceremony took place in Nairobi on World Environment Day, June 5, 1977. Participants walked from Kenyatta International Conference Center, where the newly created offices of the National Environment Secretariat were located, to the grounds popularized as Kamukunji, a park in the outskirts of the city.

Present at the ceremony were, among others, the then Mayor of the City of Nairobi Margaret Kenyatta, the then Minister for Water Development Julius Gikonyo Kiano and George Muhoho, who was then the Director of National Environment Secretariat. To make tree planting more meaningful, all Save the Land Harambee tree-planting ceremonies had a theme. This first ceremony focused on honoring deceased Kenyans who had made outstanding contributions at the community or national level. The idea was inspired by my observation of the contrasting ways with which my grandparents', parents' and my generation perceived these outstanding members of society. Unlike the former two, many in my generation marginalized them and disregarded their great achievements. This was partly as a result of colonialism, which condemned our heroes and role models and instead praised those who collaborated with them.

I felt deeply that the leaders who had sacrificed so much on our behalf were part of our history, and that they deserved our respect and honor for their extremely significant and selfless contributions. Seven trees were therefore planted in honor of Wangu wa Makeri from Murang'a, Madam Ketilili from Kilifi, Waiyaki wa Hinga from Kiambu, Nabongo Mumia from Luwero (now known as Mumias), Ole Lenana from Maasailand, Gor Mahia wuod Ogalo from Nyanza and Masaku Ngei from Machakos. Although these trees were to be nurtured by the Nairobi City Council, only two survived the neglect and hostile environment that later characterized the Kamukunji grounds. The trees now provide shade for small-scale entrepreneurs in what is now one of the busiest parts of the city (see fig. 2.5). It was the first green belt.

In September 1977, the second green belt was established when Kenya hosted the United Nations Conference on Desertification in Nairobi. At the conference, NCWK representatives focused on the problems that the ordinary rural population was facing due to desertification. As part of its contribution to the conference, NCWK organized a tree-planting activity in Naivasha, where, with the financial support of Mobil Oil of Kenya, delegates established a green belt. This was done on land owned by a cooperative of about 800 rural women from Kiambu—a district that borders Nairobi province. The event was a historic and memorable occasion for Save the Land Harambee

Fig 2.5: *One of the very first seven trees planted by members of the Green Belt Movement at Kamukunji grounds.*

and indeed for the delegates. Among those who planted trees on that day were Richard St. Barb Baker, founder of Men of the Trees, and his co-founder, Ex-Senior Chief Josiah Njonjo.

Shortly after the conference, a heightened national campaign followed that aimed at informing the public of the dangers of desertification and the necessary actions that needed to be taken at the community level to fight the process. This was done through the mass media and oral communication. As a result, many women's groups responded positively, and Save the Land Harambee began to spread quickly in various parts of the country. As interest in tree planting kept growing steadily, more farmers and public institutions, such as schools and churches, became eager to participate. In addition, invitations to tree-planting ceremonies began to trickle into the NCWK office from all over the country.

Members of the committee on Environment and Habitat also became fully involved in the project. One exemplary member who enthusiastically introduced a very successful tree-planting campaign in her home area, known as Naaro in Kandara, was the late Priscilla Ng'endo Mereka. Within a few years of the tree-planting campaign she had mobilized thousands of women to become tree planters and, in the process, changed the landscape of the area. Sadly, she passed away in 1996, but the entire community was full of praise for her. A tree was planted at her graveside to symbolize her concern for the environment and the determination of the rest of the community to carry their shared vision forward.

The women of Naaro narrate stories of the difficult past, when they used to walk long distances to fetch or purchase wood fuel and then slowly walk home carrying backbreaking loads. They also talk of the times when they had to change their diets because there was not enough fuel to cook with. Today, however, they proudly tell how they can quickly obtain sufficient supplies of wood fuel at no cost since it is now available on their farms. They also acknowledge a decline in soil erosion, the return of wildlife to their farms (especially birds and small mammals), and the benefits of cleaner air and shade. The men are grateful and full of praise for the women because of the wonderful work that they have done for the community.

As the campaign progressed, farmers persistently requested more seedlings to the point where their demand was more than NCWK could provide. Until then, Save the Land Harambee had produced its own seedlings at the NCWK headquarters or received them from the local forester, since the Department of Forestry was the only organization with an established network of tree nurseries throughout the country. In search of a solution to the shortage of seedlings, I paid a visit to the Conservator of Forests, Onesmus Mburu. I explained to Mburu our intention to plant fifteen (15) million trees throughout the country, since that was Kenya's population at the time and our motto was, "One person—One tree." Mburu burst into laughter. Because he was certain that our goal was unachievable, he quickly promised to provide all the seedlings that we would require at no charge. In less than a year, he unfortunately had to break his promise because he said we had distributed more seedlings than he could afford to give away for free. It was then our turn to laugh as he demanded payment for all the seedlings that we picked from the forestry department.

During those early days, the forestry department was very supportive of our work and we considered ourselves their helpers. With time, however, Save the Land Harambee became more effective than the forestry department due to the direct contact that it had established with farmers. Unfortunately, this resulted in hostility from the forestry department and indeed the office of the President. Some farmers were intimidated and discouraged from planting trees with Save the Land Harambee.

Despite the hostility, we continued to use government nurseries as a source of seedlings, though some logistical problems arose: First, government tree nurseries were usually located in close proximity to natural water sources that were not easily reached without vehicles. Many areas also lacked all-weather roads, and, since most farmers did not own or have access to vehicles and the government would not provide the required transport, farmers had to walk long distances to collect the few hundred seedlings that Save the Land Harambee was able to pay for. This was an extremely unsustainable method of seedling distribution.

Secondly, until quite recently no follow-up work was done by the forestry department to ensure that the seedlings they distributed actually survived. In a society where some of those in authority assume that they are not subject to question, especially by those ranked below them, procedures frequently get implemented inefficiently. Although it took the department awhile, we note that follow-ups have now been incorporated into their methodology. Perhaps they learned from our own procedure. Thirdly, NCWK was running out of funds to purchase the seedlings from the government tree nurseries.

Faced with these problems, it was decided that NCWK would encourage existing women's groups to join Save the Land Harambee and establish their own tree nurseries from which community members could obtain seedlings. In order to raise money to reach out to the women's groups and encourage them to establish tree nurseries, a fund-raising campaign was launched that appealed to members of the public to support Save the Land

Harambee. Unfortunately, very few people responded. Perhaps they, too, considered tree planting the responsibility of the government or were not fully aware of the urgent need to intensify it. One of the very few local companies that responded to the appeal was Mobil Oil (Kenya) through its chairman, Kamau Muniu, and personnel manager, E.D. Muriuki. They ensured that we obtained a grant to establish a tree nursery in Nairobi. Although the grant was not a large sum, it gave us the boost we needed to launch our own tree nurseries. When we approached the women's groups, many of them quickly embraced the idea of establishing their own tree nurseries on their farms or on public lands.

Save the Land Harambee then organized seminars to which government foresters were invited to teach the basics of tree nursery management to the women. Since the foresters were mostly training semi-literate women on issues of forestry, Save the Land Harambee felt that the foresters needed to teach using a semi-formal approach so as to make the concepts comprehensible. Unfortunately, the foresters insisted on using technical terms to describe the gradient of the land, the entry point of the sun's rays, the depth of the seedbed, the content of gravel, the type of soil and the specialized tools and inputs needed to run a successful tree nursery. It quickly became apparent that the women would be unable to implement what they had learned.

Then came the revolution. The women decided to do away with the professional approach to forestry and instead use their common sense! After all, they had for a long time successfully cultivated various crops on their farms. What was so difficult about applying this knowledge to tree planting? The campaign encouraged them to use their traditional skills, wisdom and plain common—and perhaps women—sense. They were encouraged to look for seeds in their neighborhoods, propagate trees that met their basic needs, replenish indigenous trees and protect the local biodiversity. The women quickly became very innovative and used techniques that would have been completely unacceptable to professional foresters. Indeed at one point, the foresters complained that the women were adulterating their profession! Women substituted broken pots for seedbeds, used granaries or any raised ground to keep seeds and seedlings away from domestic animals and learned to observe the flowering cycle of plants so they could harvest seeds, and also how to differentiate weeds from seedlings.

Twenty years down the road, the women have gained many skills and techniques that they continue to share among themselves. They have become self-reliant in tree planting and the foresters are now the first to acknowledge and applaud their accomplishments. Many women have indeed become foresters without diplomas (*see fig. 2.6*)!

Because of the great interest that the community members showed for tree planting, a local tree-planting strategy was developed for public land. This involved the planting of seedlings in rows of at least one thousand so as to form green belts of trees. These "belts" had the advantages of providing shade and windbreaks, facilitating soil conservation, improving the aesthetic beauty of the landscape and providing habitats for birds and small animals. During these local tree-planting ceremonies, community members usually turned out in large numbers. To conceptualize this fast-paced activity of creating belts of trees to adorn the naked land, the name *Green Belt Movement* was used.

There are numerous reasons why communities have continued to embrace the idea of tree planting. One is that in traditional times, both the women and men practiced farming,

Fig 2.6: Women "foresters without diplomas."

though they grew different crops. The women were responsible for cultivating annual crops, which they stored in granaries, while men were in charge of perennial crops like yams, cassava and bananas, which were "stored" on the farm. As times changed and the social structure of the African communities was interfered with by the colonial system, the women gradually took up the men's roles because many men began to move to urban areas for formal employment. However, the absence of many men from the farms did not mean that they had given up their roles. Therefore, when the men saw the productive work that the women were doing with tree planting, they too wanted to join in. And it was easy for them to do so without feeling that they were in conflict with tradition since the planting of trees to provide homesteads with wood fuel and building materials was really their responsibility.

A second reason for the positive response from rural communities was that seedlings were issued to them free of charge. This was necessary because many of them could not afford to add the expense for extensive tree planting to their budgets. But since they were issued free of charge, people came out in large numbers to collect the seedlings. Members of the women's groups did much of the necessary extension work to ensure that the trees were planted and that they survived.

As interest and dedication grew in various communities, so did the Green Belt Movement, and by 1999, 6,000 tree nurseries had been established in 26 districts, though some of them were not performing optimally.

The history of the Green Belt Movement would be incomplete without some reference to the National Council of Women of Kenya (NCWK), in which the project was conceived and nurtured.

NCWK has an interesting background that deserves to be discussed, especially because it is the forum through which many women became part of the women's movement in Kenya. To understand the need to create it in 1964 it is important to keep in mind that, prior to Kenya's independence, women's organizations—like all other institutions—operated along segregated racial and professional lines in a form of mild apartheid. At independence, these political vestiges of a divided society had to be abandoned. Therefore, the various women's organizations in the country decided to unite to forge a common front through which common issues and objectives could be promoted, especially those concerning women. NCWK became that common front.

Several of the organizations that qualified for immediate affiliation with NCWK were either professional, quasi-professional, quasi-religious or communal. Many had been established as branches of foreign organizations based either in Great Britain or in the United States of America. Organizations working for Asian women were also affiliated with NCWK. The only organization that represented African women was the Maendeleo ya Wanawake Organization (MYWO). Directly translated from Kiswahili, the title *Maendeleo ya Wanawake* means "Development (or Progress) for Women."

The Maendeleo ya Wanawake Organization was itself established, packaged and managed by wives of British administrators during the Mau Mau struggle. The main reason for its establishment was to preoccupy and control Kikuyu women in Central province so as to deny them time for other issues, such as paying the Mau Mau freedom fighters secret visits to provide them with food and information on what the colonial government was planning. MYWO also "rehabilitated" women who converted from the Mau Mau struggle to become British government collaborators. Of course Central province and the Kikuyu community in general was largely pro-Mau Mau and was therefore considered to be against the British government.

Much later, and especially when the suppression of the Mau Mau movement appeared to be succeeding and talks of independence were underway, the British women handed over the management of MYWO to Kenyan women. Among its first African leaders were women who had been serving as employees of the organization in various capacities (e.g. as community development officers).

By 1963, Maendeleo ya Wanawake was headed by an African woman and had opened its doors to all African women. Membership was, inevitably, mostly from Central province, though women from almost all communities were represented in the organization. NCWK had become a forum where African women could meet to discuss their future in a post-colonial Kenya.

Therefore, they rallied around it to negotiate their new relationship with other women's organizations in an independent Kenya. One of the major concessions that Maendeleo ya Wanawake successfully negotiated for at the NCWK was an increase in its votes, since it represented the majority of the women in the country. Therefore, while other organizations remained with three votes each, Maendeleo ya Wanawake was granted ten votes.

Partly in the spirit of the post-independent ambiance for reconciliation, peace and co-operation, the chairman of NCWK was always an African woman from Maendeleo ya Wanawake. The European and Asian women were content with providing support rather than leadership.

As the badges of leadership in various organizations affiliated with NCWK were passed on from European to African women, it was noted that, though there were a few Luo and Luhya women, most of the African women in the organizations were Kikuyus. For instance, Margaret Kagure Mugo represented YWCA, Priscilla Ng'endo Mereka represented the Presbyterian Woman's Guild, Jane Kiano, Wangui Mwihia, Wanjiru Mwatha and others represented MYWO and Eddah Gachukia was a nominated Member of Parliament and had been a member of MYWO. Mary Kamau, and later Evelyn Karungari Mungai, represented the Business and Professional Women, while Rose Waruhiu and I represented the Kenya Association of University Women.

3: THE OVERALL GOAL, VALUES AND PROJECTS

As the Green Belt Movement continued to engage women's groups in its tree-planting campaign, efforts toward averting desertification were intensified, although the challenge was, and is still, enormous. GBM was, however, not only interested in promoting its projects to communities but also aimed at sensitizing them to become custodians of their surrounding environment. Therefore, the overall goal of GBM in Phase I was to raise the consciousness of community members to a level that would drive them to do what was right for the environment because their hearts had been touched and their minds convinced—popular opinion notwithstanding.

Since GBM was aware that there was need for commitment in environmental conservation, it encouraged its members to embrace the following values implicitly:

1. Love for environment conservation
2. Self and community empowerment
3. Volunteerism
4. Strong sense of belonging to a community of Greens
5. Accountability, transparency and honesty

To effectively raise people's consciousness about the environment, it was necessary to assist them to practice ways through which they could still meet their felt needs while simultaneously conserving the environment. To this end, GBM established the tree-planting campaign (or project). With time, other projects were initiated to address needs either arising out of the tree-planting campaign or in response to new environmental and/or developmental needs. The GBM projects in Phase I were therefore as follows:

1. Tree-planting campaign
2. Food security and water harvesting at household level
3. Civic education
4. Advocacy
5. Green Belt Safari
6. Pan-African training workshops

The GBM Phase I projects were all run as pilot projects with the exception of the tree-planting campaign and the Pan-African training workshops. The Pan-African workshops were conducted as pilot schemes from 1986 to 1988 but were developed into a full project in 1998.

Each of these projects will now be discussed in turn.

I. TREE-PLANTING CAMPAIGN

As women's groups joined in, the GBM tree-planting campaign grew and spread into many districts—reaching communities such as the Kikuyu, Kamba, Kisii, Luhya, Luo, Meru, Embu, Samburu and Taita; the Maasai and Samburu also participated but to a lesser extent (*see fig. 3.1*). The campaign had the following as its objectives:

i. *To help community members establish a sustainable source of wood fuel*

In many parts of the less industrialized and less-consuming world, more than 90 percent of the rural population are poor and therefore depend on inexpensive and readily available forms of fuel (e.g. grain stalks, wood fuel, cow dung, etc.) for cooking and warming their homes. The use of these fuels is not without shortcomings, two of which are mentioned below.

First, when in low supply, these fuels have to be utilized sparingly. Consequently, as was earlier explained, families are sometimes forced to change their diets to foods that require relatively little energy to cook. In many cases, this is done without regard to, or knowledge of, how the changes affect the overall quality of the diet.

Secondly, in places where wood fuel is gathered but not replenished, the sources near the homesteads are quickly exhausted. This forces the gatherers, who are mostly women, to trek increasingly longer distances to gather the fuel. This is an exerting and time-consuming exercise. Furthermore, in areas where wood fuel is gathered from forests, local biodiversity gradually becomes threatened.

The tree-planting project addressed such problems by encouraging communities to plant trees to replenish what they cut in order to maintain a consistent supply, and also to use energy-saving technologies (*see fig. 3.2*). They were urged to plant various types of trees in close proximity to their homesteads to avoid the long treks, conserve the local biodiversity and improve their diets with the produce from fruit trees. As a rule of

Fig 3.1: Samburu women working at their tree nursery in Maralal.

Fig 3.2: Miricu women demonstrating wood-saving technology.

thumb, GBM members were asked to plant two seedlings for every tree felled.

ii. To generate income for rural women

Because of their pressing daily needs and relatively low income, many people in the rural areas carry out small income-generating activities, and the tree-planting campaign was one such activity. After women's groups issued seedlings to their communities free of charge, they were required to conduct a follow-up (i.e. extension services) after the first and third month to ascertain survival of the seedlings. In order to compensate them for the time that they spent tending to the nurseries and doing extension work, GBM purchased all of the seedlings issued by the groups that were surviving in the third month.

This way, the women's groups gained financially. All community members who planted trees benefited from an increased wood fuel supply and enriched soil (through agroforestry), and from the sale of timber. Even those in the community who did not plant trees still gained from the improved environment and scenic beauty.

iii. To promote environmental consciousness among the youth

Since the youth are the decision makers of the future, it was deemed important to expose and involve them in issues of environmental conservation. In this respect, GBM sensitized the youth to the environment by establishing public tree nurseries in schools. Through these nurseries, students were taught the importance of environmental conservation and were encouraged to involve themselves in tree planting. Once sensitized, some of the youth further spread the message of conservation to their families and beyond (see fig. 3.3).

Fig 3.3: An example of a public green belt at Kariua Primary School.

iv. To empower people at the grass roots

In Phase I, the Green Belt Movement depended on those at the grass roots to carry out the work on the ground. Therefore, it was found increasingly important for the headquarters to delegate some of the managerial duties to tree-nursery members to increase efficiency. These duties included record keeping, accounting for funds, decision making on tree nursery management, organizing activities (e.g. meetings) and providing leadership.

Community members who carried out these duties gained a lot of experience and are now applying these skills in other capacities, including positions of leadership within the community. GBM views individual and communal empowerment as an important aspect of development because it is, in many cases, the mind-set from which people begin to realize their potential.

v. To demonstrate the capacity of women in development

In a nation where women's roles are commonly perceived as subordinate, the Movement found it important to raise awareness—both in rural and urban areas—of the willingness, ability and capacity of women to play leading roles in communal, regional and national development. With the visible positive impact created by the women's groups, many men have gained respect and high regard for the women, and others have joined GBM groups and are proud to be part of their conservation effort.

vi. To curb soil erosion

Land is one of Kenya's most important national resources. Its fertile topsoil ought to be considered a very valuable resource, especially because it continues to play a major role in sustaining the economy through agriculture. However, little immediate and economic value is attached to soil per se, perhaps because the effects of losing it are gradual and have not been felt yet—at least not by the masses.

During the rainy seasons, thousands of tons of topsoil are eroded from Kenya's countryside by rivers and washed into the ocean and lakes. Additionally, soil is lost through wind erosion in areas where the land is devoid of vegetative cover. Losing topsoil should be considered analogous to losing territory to an invading enemy. And indeed, if any country were so threatened, it would mobilize all available resources, including a heavily armed military, to protect the priceless land. Unfortunately, the loss of soil through these elements has yet to be perceived with such urgency in Kenya.

Soil erosion is precipitated by a number of factors, including:

(a) Indiscriminate deforestation and clearing of vegetative cover from the land surface
(b) Destruction of catchment areas
(c) Cultivation along riverbeds, slopes and marginal lands using inappropriate methods
(d) Poorly planned construction of infrastructure (e.g. roads)

Fortunately, soil erosion can easily be checked by applying simple preventive measures.

GBM trained community members to apply inexpensive techniques such as planting appropriate species of trees, maintaining vegetative cover on the land, creating windbreaks, digging trenches, constructing terraces, making cut-off drains and protecting forests and catchment areas from indiscriminate exploitation.

vii. To disseminate information on environment conservation

In order to train communities to become good custodians of the environment, GBM found it crucial for them to understand the causes and effects of environmental problems. Through such forums as seminars and meetings, many environment-related problems were identified and discussed.

These problems include sustained hunger, malnutrition, widespread poverty, unemployment, overpopulation, energy crises, soil erosion, lack of clean drinking water, lack of building materials, lack of animal fodder, drought and desertification. Out of the discussions, problems that could be tackled through tree planting were listed and possible actions outlined for the participants to implement.

The Tree-Planting Methodology

As the tree-planting campaign grew over the years, its methodology was reviewed severally for purposes of efficiency and effectiveness. For simplicity, it was termed the Ten-Step Procedure.

The steps are as follows:

1. GBM headquarters and field staff disseminate information on the importance of tree planting to communities.
2. Field staff facilitates the formation of groups.
3. Groups register with the GBM headquarters.
4 Groups prepare their tree-nursery sites.
5. Groups send monthly reports to the headquarters.
6. Groups announce to their communities that seedlings are ready for issuing and ask those interested to dig holes.
7. Holes are checked by group members.
8. Seedlings are issued only to those who dug holes properly.
9. The first verification of seedling survival is conducted by group members and information sent to the headquarters.
10. The second verification of seedling survival is conducted and information is sent to the headquarters. If acceptable, GBM purchases the seedlings.

This procedure proved useful in guiding GBM staff and the community members to establish tree nurseries (steps 1–4) and operate them (steps 5–10). To increase efficiency at the local level, the ten-step procedure was translated into local languages. An in-depth discussion of this methodology is given in Chapter Ten.

2. FOOD SECURITY AND WATER HARVESTING AT THE HOUSEHOLD LEVEL

Over the years, food production in Africa has gradually decreased in yield, so much so that in some regions famine is a recurrent phenomenon, while in others, Africans are regularly importing food. In addition, the number of malnourished adults and children is increasing. Among the leading causes of poor crop yield are the over-utilization of land and loss of topsoil.

In response to these impediments, GBM established a pilot project in two sub-locations in Kiharu Murang'a and urged the farmers in those areas to adopt food-security and water-harvesting practices. To ensure that the project reached a large majority of community members, it was conducted at the household level.

Though food security and water harvesting are closely intertwined, they are discussed separately here so as to highlight the significance of each, beginning with food security.

2.1 Food Security at the Household Level

A household can be considered food secure when its members have access to adequate and quality food at all times. Unfortunately, this is not the case for many households.

The project therefore aimed at enhancing household food security through the following objectives:

- Promotion of sustainable farming methods
- Community education on food production and nutrition

2.1.1 Promoting Sustainable Farming Methods

As stated earlier, it is the unsustainable use of farmland that has led to the gradual decrease in yield of many food and cash crops.

GBM, therefore, educated farmers on how to maintain the fertility of their land to ensure its long-term use. Information was conveyed to the farmers through seminars and meetings in which food-security problems and solutions were deliberated. In addition, demonstration gardens were used to illustrate to participants the various farming techniques that were discussed in the meetings.

The issues highlighted in the promotion of sustainable farming included:

(a) Organic Farming

Over the years, many farmers have ignored organic and other sustainable methods of farming because they are convinced that chemical fertilizers are more appropriate. Unfortunately, such misplaced notions handicap them in a number of ways.

First, because their finances have been mismanaged by cooperatives and other agents for so long, many farmers are poor, yet fertilizers are expensive. Therefore, some farmers opt to purchase relatively small quantities of fertilizer that only contribute to minimal quantity and quality of yield. Secondly, with the current economic world order it is unlikely that the prices of these fertilizers will drop and thus become more affordable. Thirdly, many farmers are unaware that chemical fertilizers inhibit the regenerative capacity of the soil, thereby undermining sustainable farming and causing further land impoverishment.

To address these obstacles, GBM promoted organic farming techniques to farmers through seminars and meetings since these measures could inexpensively maintain soil fertility, reduce input costs and increase yields. The techniques that were promoted included the use of animal manure, mulching, composting and agroforestry.

(b) Crop Rotation

This refers to the growing of different specified crops on the same piece of land, in successive seasons. The key point in crop rotation is that as various crops are grown from season to season, they take up from and add nutrients to the soil in a manner that minimizes the net change in the nutrient content of the soil over time. This approach is beneficial because it does not require inputs over and above what a farmer would ordinarily use. GBM has encouraged farmers to rotate their crops and, where necessary, increase the variety of crops that they cultivate so as to make the process of soil replenishment more effective.

(c) Provide training on proper farming techniques

Low yield in food production is also partly due to unskilled farming. In Africa, a large proportion of food is produced by small-scale farmers, who are mostly rural women. Although their lack of skill was noted years ago, the extension programs set up to assist them have been ineffective because many extension officers never visit the farms to supervise the types of crops being cultivated and the methods being applied. Instead, the extension officers prefer to spend time in their offices performing the so-called white-collar jobs while the land continues to be underutilized, improperly cultivated and degraded.

Through seminars and on-site meetings, GBM conveyed information on proper farming techniques to farmers. Additionally, practical training sessions were held at demonstration gardens to ensure that farmers fully understood the concepts being presented.

(d) Promote food production at the household level

Since the 1970s, it has been noted that many farmers have gradually increased the acreage of their land under cash-crop farming at the expense of subsistence farming. At first glance, this appears logical since farmers can use some of the income gained from the cash crops to purchase nutritious foods for their families and invest the rest elsewhere. However, because of gross underpayment, they find themselves unable to properly feed their households. Also, when there is drought or flooding, little income is generated.

For these reasons, and especially the latter, GBM encouraged farmers to practice both cash and subsistence farming so as to ensure household food security. They were also encouraged to plant indigenous food crops (roots, cereals, legumes and vegetables) for added nutrient value and conservation of local biological diversity.

2.1.2 Community Education on Food Production and Nutrition

This was a felt need of the rural women because their children suffered from malnutrition even though the community was considered affluent. Therefore, GBM addressed this issue by educating communities on the value of traditional foods and wisdom. It did this with the following plan:

(a) Promote indigenous food crops

Many of the indigenous food crops—such as tubers—are only consumed in small quantities in many households today. This is partly because their nutritional value is not well understood by consumers despite the fact that many of them are higher in nutrients than processed exotic foods.

In an effort to promote these foods, GBM members were informed of their nutritional value and also of the various ways of cultivating and cooking them. They were also urged to farm indigenous foods because of their ability to withstand harsh environmental conditions.

In addition, GBM promoted indigenous food crops through the introduction of food security programs in schools. A pilot project was introduced at Kanyariri Secondary School in which indigenous foods were grown and consumed by the students. This was a strategy to help the youth appreciate the nutritional value of these foods as well as improve their diets since they had previously relied on "fast food." It turned out to be a success, especially because both the parents and students appreciated the value of the food.

(b) Encourage the preservation of traditional knowledge and wisdom regarding agriculture

In African traditional societies, a lot of knowledge and wisdom regarding agricultural practices and the value of various plants have been passed on from generation to generation. The organization recognized the value of this information, more so because some of it is still applicable today. GBM therefore encouraged its members to preserve, utilize and share this knowledge with other community members. Some have already documented their information because they realize its immense value.

2.2 Water Harvesting

GBM perceives the concept of water harvesting from two perspectives—as a farming technique and as a method of increasing water supply for the household.

The techniques of harvesting water in farming were taught in seminars and at demonstration gardens. Some of the techniques discussed were simple damming, benching, mulching, pitting, cut-off drains, terracing, manure application, cover-cropping, double-digging, contour farming, furrowing and agroforestry. These techniques serve to hold water (as reservoirs on the farm), slow the rate of run-off water so that it can permeate into the soil, loosen it and increase its permeability.

Regarding the harvesting of rainwater for household use, GBM encouraged those who had corrugated iron sheets on the roofs of their houses to direct the water into storage tanks. This way, several liters of water could be harvested and stored for use at a time of scarcity. Unfortunately, corrugated iron sheets and water tanks are expensive, so not everybody can afford to harvest water in this way. However, community activities such as revolving funds enable people to purchase them.

3. CIVIC EDUCATION

Recognizing the need to build a strong civil society of environmental conservationists to enhance and preserve a quality environment, GBM established a pilot civic education project.

This was carried out through seminars held both at the Green Belt Movement Training Center in Nairobi and in the villages. The seminars, which were interactive in nature, ensured that the experiences and concerns of the participants formed the basis for discussions and recommendations.

The main issues addressed were as follows:

i. Governance

Here, the relationship between governance and the quality of the environment was established. Discussions were especially focused on the linkages between poor governance and environmental degradation since this is more applicable to Kenya's current condition. Aspects of poor governance that were discussed included corruption, mismanagement of national resources (e.g. forests), loss of biodiversity and lack of essential services such as health care, education and clean drinking water.

ii. Culture and Spirituality

This component addressed the significance of cultural and spiritual values since they linked people with their roots, God and environment. This was necessary because the cultural values and systems of indigenous Kenyans were eroded, trivialized and deliberately destroyed in the process of colonization. As a result, many people are less appreciative of the environment because they now perceive it as a commodity to be privatized and exploited.

Even after colonization, it is unfortunate that cultural values still continue to be suppressed today in the name of modernization, civilization and Christianity. The restoration of positive spiritual and cultural values is important since these contribute toward restoration of individual self-confidence, empowerment and identity. This restoration is also important in the protection of indigenous biological diversity, knowledge, practices and wisdom.

iii. Africa's Development Crisis

This issue addressed the crises faced in the development process of Africa from the perspective of those at the grass roots rather than from that of the leaders at the top. The issues discussed here included poverty, unemployment, population pressure and environmental degradation. Through this, people perceived how their actions enhanced or retarded development and were challenged to take appropriate action where necessary

iv. *Human and Environmental Rights*

In the seminars, issues of women's rights and economic injustice—especially those affecting farmers—were addressed.

With respect to economic injustice, part of the problem is that the government continues to allow the politically well-connected to use dubious means to generate income at the expense of local entrepreneurs. Furthermore, the unregulated opening of national borders to foreign investors—who have more capital, knowledge and skills compared with their local competitors—does not serve the local business sector. Rather than compete, local entrepreneurs are pushed to the periphery of their own economy. A good government should protect the interests of its people. Unfortunately, the small-scale farmers, especially those who reside in constituencies that are dominated by opposition political parties, are the most oppressed and exploited citizens. The seminars helped farmers gain an understanding of how they were being exploited so that they could more effectively advocate for justice. Indeed, they have already begun.

Some communities still oppose efforts by women to acquire basic human rights and freedoms regarding reproduction. They deny women the rights of self-determination and self-fulfillment. As long as this prevails, it is difficult to control the rate of population growth and realize sustainable development. Just like men, women must be given the opportunity to determine their destinies. During the seminars, these issues were raised and deliberated upon. Both men and women were encouraged to hold open dialogues amongst themselves as a way of searching for workable solutions to the issue.

4. ADVOCACY

Because of the gross mismanagement that prevailed in the government in the late eighties and early nineties, GBM begun to advocate against environmental and human rights abuse. Though this was a pilot project, its activities were effective.

One such activity was the effort in 1989 that stopped the construction of a 62-story building in Nairobi in Uhuru Park. Another activity was the support that GBM gave in 1992 to the mothers of "political prisoners" who were demonstrating in Uhuru Park for the release of their sons. The demonstrations gave rise to the Release Political Prisoners (RPP) pressure group and the creation of Freedom Corner.

Also, at the advent of multiparty politics in Kenya, a group of pro-democracy activists, including GBM, advocated for unity of the Opposition through a body known as the Middle Ground Group (MGG).

Since the ruling party had governed the country poorly and in a dictatorial manner, a change in leadership was deemed important. The MGG strongly advised the opposition presidential candidates to unite and field one candidate against the ruling party in the 1992 elections. Unfortunately, the candidates ignored that advice and all lost to the ruling party.

GBM was also involved in the Jubilee 2000 campaign, which continues to advocate for the cancellation of the unpayable debts that the less developed countries, many of which are in Africa, owe to the rich in the North. GBM conducted seminars on the subject and encouraged the clergy to promote the campaign in their churches.

Advocacy efforts were also directed against corruption, especially in relation to public land and open spaces that the government continues to illegally allocate to private developers (now commonly known as "land grabbers"). The most prominent of these efforts was the advocacy to save Karura, Mt. Kenya and Kafiru-ini forests (*see figs. 3.4 and 3.5*).

Initially, it was only GBM and a few other concerned parties that would organize advocacy campaigns against such developers. Currently, however, members of the public have become increasingly involved in advocacy because they have seen its positive impact. People are now quick to take to the streets to condemn greedy developers when they attempt to grab land. Citizens are gradually becoming empowered.

Advocacy efforts even spread into some of the rural areas where GBM members demonstrated against land grabbers and those destroying forests. Such valiant advocacy work was demonstrated in 1999 at Kahuro in Murang'a, Kitale, Embu, Meru and Nyandarua. Rather than lead the way for the local people, GBM only provided support and withdrew as the local people performed their demonstrations. Since most of the participants had undergone civic education, their actions demonstrated the importance of such education as well as the importance of community empowerment in development.

When there occurred communal conflicts in parts of the Rift Valley in 1991, GBM assisted victims by drawing attention to their plight, both nationally and internationally. GBM also provided civic education seminars and material support to the victims.

5. Green Belt Safaris

For several years, various donors in industrialized countries have continued to fund development projects in the less industrialized nations. For profit-making programs, sustainability has not been

Fig 3.4: *Advocacy for Karura Forest.*

Fig 3.5: Demonstrating on the streets of Nairobi against land-grabbing.

of major concern since this is achievable through effective management. However, the donor community continues to express
concern over the sustainability of non-profit programs that
wholly rely on them for funding. The Green Belt Movement is
one such organization, since for much of its existence it has fully
depended on external funding. This is now changing through the
formation of a business development department that is focused
on establishing initiatives through which GBM can earn an
income and begin to financially sustain itself.

One such initiative is the Green Belt Safaris (GBS), an eco-
safari operating company based in Nairobi. The intention is to
offer community-based and other eco-tourism packages through
which environmental conservation and community development can be promoted. Though it is still operating as a pilot, a
number of successful feasibility safaris have been conducted

that have indicated that the program is now ready to move to full-scale operation.

6. PAN-AFRICAN TRAINING WORKSHOPS

The environmental problems that GBM addresses through its projects are not unique to Kenya but can be found among several communities in various countries, especially the less developed ones. By using the approach of the Green Belt Movement in other countries, it is possible to alleviate some of these problems. The replication of GBM and promotion of green consciousness in other African nations was the main objective of the Pan-African Training Workshops in Phase I. Full details of the project are given in Chapter Eleven, where the replication of GBM is discussed.

4: THE ORGANIZATION'S STRUCTURE

The structure and management of the Green Belt Movement have evolved with the growth of the organization such that, over the years, they have become more complex and extensive. Though there is much that can be stated about the growth of GBM and its framework, the following discussion is limited to the structure of the organization from the time Phase I reached maturity to its end.

In Phase I, the organization had staff members both at the headquarters and in the field. They all worked in one of the following sections or departments:

- Project Management
- Administration
- Finance
- Coordination

Except for project management, all staff in the other departments were based at the headquarters. Details of these departments follow.

Project Management

For all projects, with the exception of the tree-planting program, the management was organized as shown below:

PROJECT OFFICER

ASSISTANT PROJECT OFFICER

SUPPORT STAFF

The role of the Project Officer was to oversee the project at all stages of its development. In the planning stages, this involved developing a project design that included formulation of the main objectives, strategies and activities. Once the plan was approved, the project officer was also responsible for implementing the project and conducting periodic evaluations.

The Assistant Project Officer played a supporting role to the Project Officer in all aspects of the project. The Support Staff played an important role especially in the implementation and evaluation of projects, since they too carried out several tasks that, though relatively simple, ensured the smooth operation of projects. Their contributions in evaluations were also useful. As earlier mentioned, the tree-planting program was the core GBM project in Phase I; consequently it had the most elaborate structure, as shown below:

PROJECT OFFICER

ASSISTANT PROJECT OFFICER

REGIONAL MONITORS

MONITORS

TREE-NURSERY GROUPS

- Promoters
- Mini-advisors
- Tree-nursery attendants

In many communities in Kenya today, people are familiar with the Green Belt Movement regardless of whether they are active members. This is due to a number of factors, one of which is information dissemination. At the grass roots, information dissemination was carried out by promoters who were also members of the tree-nursery groups. They highlighted the threats that the environment faced and proposed tree planting as a possible solution.

Those who expressed interest were referred to the local mini-advisor, who instructed and assisted them in initiating their tree nursery group through the first four steps of the ten-step procedure. To perform the daily chores around the tree nursery, each group engaged a tree-nursery attendant.

The tree-nursery groups were overseen by monitors, who were a group of extension workers, based at the headquarters. They were responsible for data collection and evaluation of tree nurseries, training of group members and field staff, recommending tools for groups, and financial compensation for the extension work done by the women. The monitors were in turn supervised by regional monitors, who worked closely with the project officer and the assistant.

Administration

The department comprising the Board, Executive Committee and Secretariat was responsible for the management of the GBM head office and projects. In addition, it maintained donor and community relations.

Finance

The finance department was responsible for the management of GBM funds and assets. It produced annual audited reports of all funds that were granted to the organization by its donors.

Coordination

The main tasks related to this office included sustenance of the vision of the organization, conceptualizing new projects and writing proposals, overseeing the progress made by existing projects, writing both financial and project reports, managing personnel, convening Board and Annual General meetings and maintaining international relations.

5: FUNDING

I t is only in the last few years that the Green Belt Movement began venturing into income-generating activities as a way of strengthening the sustainability of the organization. For most of its existence, it has depended on funding from various donors for all its operations.

The funding process in the organization has changed and grown since its establishment. As Envirocare, the organization was supported through the author's personal funds. As Save the Land Harambee, it first received small donations from individuals who usually sponsored between one and three trees, but later obtained funds from Mobil Oil (Kenya) Ltd.

The Danish Voluntary Fund for Developing Countries, the Spirit of Stockholm Foundation and the Canadian Embassy (*see fig. 5.1*) also joined in to support what had by then become the tree-planting program of the National Council of Women of Kenya.

In order to enable GBM to expand and reach the grassroots communities, the United Nations Fund for Women (UNIFEM) donated a large amount of funds toward the tree-planting project in 1981. This support was provided through the efforts of senior women in the United Nations in New York, among them Margaret Snyder of the United States and Helvi Sipila of Finland.

Fig 5.1: *The Canadian Ambassador handing over the keys of a minibus to the chairwoman of the National Council of Women of Kenya, Eddah Gachuki, in 1979. The author (fourth left) and other members of the board look on.*

With these funds, a lot of awareness was raised, many tree-nursery groups were formed and many trees were planted.

Others who have supported the tree-planting program include NORAD, CARE-Austria, the Norwegian Forestry society, GBM-Utah (USA), Tanaka-Japan, Lady Forest of Finland, *Brigitte* (a German magazine that focuses on women's issues), the Turner Foundation and Resource Renewal Institute of California.

Rather than fund the organization as a whole, some donors prefer to fund specific GBM projects. The Pan-African training workshops is one such project that was initially funded by UNEP for three years and is now funded by Comic Relief (UK). Another is civic education, which has been funded by the Open Society Institute of the Soros Foundation, the Commission on Global

Governance, the National Endowment for Democracy, Earth Love Fund (Peace Trees), Norwegian People's Aid, the Heinrich Bohl Foundation and several individuals who have made small but very helpful donations.

Still other donors have preferred to respond to the infrastructure-related needs of the Green Belt Movement. These include the Government of Austria through CARE-Austria, which donated the property at Lang'ata, NOVIB, Steven Rockefeller of the Rockefeller Foundation and Joshua Mailman of the Sirius Business Corporation in New York City. They all donated funds for the purchase of office space for GBM in Kilimani, Nairobi.

The property at Kilimani serves as the head office while the Lang'ata property serves a training center. For six years before these centers opened, GBM had been operating from a congested space at the coordinator's home. This was because the government expelled GBM from the public offices it was occupying because of its advocacy for the conservation of Uhuru Park—an initiative that went against the business interests of some highly placed government officials. Nevertheless GBM survived, and once the office was purchased, Tudor Trust of London provided the funds to do some of the major renovations.

Other donors include GAIA Foundation (UK) and the Women's Environment and Development Organization (WEDO), based in New York City, which donated funds to GBM to help pay for publications. The late leader of WEDO, Bella Abzug, was a great promoter of women's issues, the environment and the work of GBM.

The African Development Foundation also made a major contribution by providing the funds required to film a documentary on GBM titled *The Naked Earth*, screened at the second United Nations Conference for Women in 1985 in Nairobi.

The current donors of the Green Belt Movement include NOVIB of the Netherlands, the Finnish Coalition for Environment and Development, CARE-Austria, Charity Projects of Britain and the Heinrich Bohl Foundation (of Germany).

All these donors fund tree planting, environmental education and food security—except Charity Projects, which funds the Pan-African Training Workshops, and the Heinrich Boll Foundation, which funds civic education.

Over the years, GBM has nurtured its relationships with its donors and continues to enjoy them to this day. Donors continue to play an important role in the running of GBM, although they now require, and rightly so, that the organization focus on self-sustainability. The contribution that donors have made toward the development of the organization is enormous. The Green Belt Movement will always remain grateful to them for their spirit of comradeship and the generous donations and grants, both large and small. Unfortunately, the Kenyan government was and remains a major detractor and a source of harassment and violent obstructions.

6: ACHIEVEMENTS

The Green Belt Movement has a large constituency of people at the grassroots level, most of whom are peasant men and women farmers. There are two main reasons why the majority are farmers. First, Kenya is still largely a rural economy with most people practicing subsistence agriculture. Secondly, it is easier for farmers to implement GBM activities since they work closely with the soil much more frequently than those residing in the urban centers. Therefore, many of the achievements of the organization have been made in the rural areas through farmers. In urban centers, GBM's initiatives tend to focus around advocacy, especially against the privatization of open public spaces and forests.

Each GBM project has its own achievements, which when taken together constitute the achievements of the organization. These achievements are listed below and discussed thereafter.

1. Rural forestation and reforestation
2. Creation of employment
3. Raising awareness on the importance of the environment
4. Empowerment of individuals and communities
5. Community mobilization
6. A source of inspiration

7. Raising awareness of the need to protect local biological diversity of plants and food crops
8. An improved image of women
9. Increased advocacy and networking activities
10. Increased number of agricultural tools in communities
11. Extensive documentation and recognition of the Green Belt Movement
12. Survival of the Movement despite political persecution

1. RURAL FORESTATION AND REFORESTATION

There are three major accomplishments that have been realized through rural forestation and reforestation, and they are as follows.

1.1 Increased tree cover

By June 1999, it was estimated that GBM women's group members had facilitated the planting of more than twenty million trees countrywide, and although some of these have been harvested, millions are still standing (*see fig. 6.1*).

In areas where the campaign has been successful, the increase in tree cover is impressive to the naked eye. This is the organization's most visible achievement.

1.2 A positive difference in the lives of thousands of people in the rural areas has been realized

The lives of thousands of people have been touched in a positive way. For instance, there are thousands of women who no longer walk long distances to fetch firewood because they now have trees on their farms (*see fig. 6.2*). They also save financially since they do not have to buy building and fencing materials; when in need, they fell their trees and obtain timber from them.

Fig 6.1: There has been a tremendous increase in tree cover in successful areas.

Fig 6.2: Women carrying back-breaking loads of firewood is a thing of the past in successful areas.

Many farmers have also improved the quality of their household diets through fruits from the trees. When in surplus, the fruits are sold for extra income.

1.3 Tree nursery group members have earned income for their extension work

The members of tree nurseries are responsible for the extension work—part of which is to ensure the survival of seedlings that are planted on the farms. For this, the women earn an allowance that they can use to meet some of their needs (e.g. clothing, household goods, school fees, acquisition of livestock, purchase of seeds, etc.). That has improved the quality of their lives.

2. CREATION OF EMPLOYMENT WITHIN THE MOVEMENT

When membership, which had been mostly comprised of women's groups, began to increase steadily, GBM engaged promoters and tree-nursery attendants at the tree-nursery level, and mini-advisors at the sub-location level, so as to increase the effectiveness of the tree-planting project. At its most active period, there were about 2,600 such employees working in various parts of the country.

It is important to note that these employees were considered part-time workers in the sense that they were active all year round but were not required to put in a full day's work every day. The tree-nursery attendants earned an amount equal to one-third of what was paid to the tree-nursery groups. It was reasoned that the performance of a tree nursery was a reflection of the effectiveness of their extension work. Because the Green Belt Movement had limited funds for its work, these employees did not earn very much. Therefore, to lessen their living expenses, most workers were commissioned close to their homes.

3. RAISING AWARENESS OF THE IMPORTANCE OF THE ENVIRONMENT

The Green Belt Movement has succeeded in raising public awareness of the need to protect the environment. The message of environmental conservation has not only reached millions of people in Kenya but has also extended to other parts of Africa and beyond.

In Kenya, this has translated into making environmental conservation an important issue now worth the efforts of academic and government institutions alike. For instance, the government has ordered the introduction of Environmental Studies in schools and teacher-training colleges. Also, the government introduced a Bill in Parliament for the protection of the environment and forests. Since there are indeed other actors carrying out environmental conservation initiatives, the Green Belt Movement cannot claim all the credit for this. However, the Green Belt Movement has contributed to and pioneered these changes.

Awareness of the importance of the environment has also been promoted in schools. So far, over 3,000 schools have wood-lots that were established with the involvement of students.

4. EMPOWERMENT OF INDIVIDUALS AND COMMUNITIES

Through its various projects, the Green Belt Movement has managed to empower individuals and communities. This is especially

Fig 6.3: Empowered communities take action and establish tree nurseries.

true of areas where community members have taken the GBM projects seriously and made a positive impact (see fig. 6.3).

GBM has been an outspoken NGO that continues to challenge the government on various issues, such as corruption and human rights violations. Consequently, it often finds itself at loggerheads with the powers that be. To rid itself of such pressure, the government has tried to destroy GBM through members of the local provincial administration, who have urged their constituents to dissociate themselves from GBM and its projects. However, these efforts have been unsuccessful because GBM members are aware of the benefits of the projects and also understand conservation and its role in environmental sustenance. Once empowered, people are capable of making conscious and informed decisions for self-determination.

Empowerment has also been attained through civic education. For instance, in a series of civic education seminars, coffee farmers were taught about the dubious means that were being used to swindle them of their rightful income. Armed with this information, they initiated a farmers-rights campaign for coffee growers. Though it has been a difficult struggle, they have vowed to keep applying pressure for their rights.

Women, too, have become empowered in a number of ways. It has become more evident to them that, though deprived in some aspects, they have the potential to make a difference in their communities. This has given them a great deal of confidence with which many continue to discover and develop their talents. Some have initiated group projects (e.g. revolving funds) while others have become independent leaders and decision-makers capable of addressing various community-related issues without as much assistance from GBM offices as they previously required.

5. COMMUNITY MOBILIZATION

Community empowerment often leads to community mobilization. This has been true in GBM and has occurred in a number of ways. Over the last twenty years of the tree-planting campaign, thousands of rural women were mobilized to fight against environmental degradation in their own communities. School children and various institutions also have been mobilized.

6. A SOURCE OF INSPIRATION

It has indeed taken tremendous time and effort to develop GBM into what it is today. It is therefore a privilege to know that others continue to be inspired by it. At the local level, some environmental groups have been initiated, especially by the youth, as a result of what they have experienced or read about the Green Belt Movement. It has become clear to such groups that they are custodians of their environment and that they too must play a role to ensure that their environment is cared for.

As was earlier mentioned, many communities in Africa experience similar problems and, in many cases, use similar approaches to solve them. The tree-planting campaign is an example of such an approach that has inspired some development workers. This has grown to the extent that GBM is now promoting its approach and sharing its experience with people from other parts of Africa.

University students have also found GBM to be an inspirational development initiative, to the extent that some successfully studied it for master's and Ph.D. degrees. Some interns have also had an opportunity to work for the organization and have found it a worthwhile experience.

The staff of the Green Belt Movement also feel privileged to be part of an effort that is making a difference in society. They too find it inspirational because of the continuous development and empowerment that they undergo. Through these experiences, some have even developed into trainers. All who have been committed to the organization and to one or more of its projects have found the task of development challenging but also very inspiring and rewarding.

7. RAISING AWARENESS OF THE NEED TO PROTECT LOCAL BIOLOGICAL DIVERSITY OF PLANTS AND FOOD CROPS

Both the colonial and the current education system promoted exotic biological diversity of trees and crops at the expense of indigenous species (*see fig. 6.4*). This is because the exotic species of trees such as eucalyptus (from the southern hemisphere) and

Fig 6.4: *Yams are some of the indigenous food crops needing conservation.*

the pines (from the temperate zones of the northern hemisphere) were (and are still) promoted for rapid economic returns.

Even in forestry schools and research institutions, exotic species continue to receive preference over local ones. Convincing farmers to plant indigenous trees has been challenging. However, with persuasion and constant education, farmers have begun to appreciate the short and long-term economic value of the indigenous trees and have even began to search for these species on their own.

In addition, the organization has raised the consciousness of several people regarding the need to conserve local biological diversity. This has been done mainly through seminars in which the interdependence of the various components of nature are discussed. Community members now appreciate this, especially in areas where tree planting has succeeded, because they have noticed the return of birds and small mammals to their areas. Some have formed mini-forests on their farms with a diverse range of indigenous trees.

8. An Improved Image of Women

The impact of the Movement's activities in rural communities, where the efforts are most visible, has been positive because women have done the work. The success of the Green Belt Movement is the success of the women of Kenya, and, while they may not be publicly recognized or rewarded appropriately, they are proud of their work and know it is for the common good of their community.

Through the Movement, they have been able to demonstrate their creativity and leadership skills. Indeed, many men have been positively influenced by the women and have followed their example through the initiation of their own tree nurseries.

The Green Belt Movement is an example of a successful development project *by* the people rather than *for* the people. It was structured to avoid the urge to work *for* rather than *with* them. This approach is empowering the local people.

9. Increased Advocacy and Networking Activities

From the time the organization was formed, advocacy and networking were perceived to be important components of the tree-planting campaign. However, this was also the period when Kenya was governed through a single party, which became increasingly corrupt and intolerant to criticisms from the public on its mismanagement of natural resources, which included the destruction of catchment areas and the encroachment and privatization of forests, open spaces and parks. The more the destruction of the environment increased, the more it became necessary for GBM to increase its advocacy and networking activities. GBM's efforts energized members of the public, who also took on this role and protected open spaces in their areas. In the beginning, groups and communities would invite GBM to do the advocacy, but later they became empowered enough to take on the role themselves and protect their own open spaces and public lands.

10. INCREASED NUMBER OF AGRICULTURAL TOOLS IN COMMUNITIES

Women's groups receive garden tools, fencing materials, water tanks, pipes and manure. The equipment adds to the supply of agricultural tools in communities. These have proved to be very useful not only to the group members who receive them but also to other members of communities who have few of these agricultural tools and who therefore borrow from each other.

11. EXTENSIVE DOCUMENTATION AND RECOGNITION OF THE GREEN BELT MOVEMENT

An indicator of the success and impact of the Movement is the attention that it has received. For example, several films have featured the activities of the Green Belt Movement; the best known are The Naked Earth (Green Belt Movement, 1985), Women at Work (NOVIB, 1986) and The Green Belt Movement—Kenya (Erik Allgower, 1999). The organization is also featured in The Race to Save the Planet—an environmental educational package used in colleges in the United States of America.

Additionally, many international prizes have been awarded the founder and the organization in recognition of the successes of the Green Belt Movement. These prizes include The Africa

Leadership Prize, the Goldman Environment Award, the Better World Society Award, the Right Livelihood Award, the Windstar Award and the Honors List of the National Council of Women of Kenya Award. The founder has also served as the Representative of the International Council of Women to the United Nations Environmental Programme (UNEP) and received awards of recognition from the Federation of Women Lawyers as well as honorary degrees from universities and colleges.

Many press articles have been published about the Movement, both locally and internationally. These have been encouraging, especially when one considers the numerous negative images of Africa that are presented to the world. GBM has been a sign of hope.

12. SURVIVAL OF THE MOVEMENT

Were it not for the desire of many individuals, especially those in the government of Daniel arap Moi, to see the Movement collapse, survival would not be such an appreciated achievement of the Green Belt Movement. But GBM has survived through many trials, including threats to have it banned, and the founder has been a subject of extensive vilification and ridicule in the gutter-press and through government agents.

GBM's survival is attributed to the belief by members that the campaign to plant trees was—and still is—important. Although workers at a few tree nurseries in areas dominated by KANU have been intimidated and persuaded to stop planting trees with the Movement, the larger number of women's groups have refused to be overwhelmed by overenthusiastic supporters of the government and the ruling party, which specializes in discrediting and disempowering its own citizens.

7: CONSTRAINTS

Though the Green Belt Movement has realized many accomplishments, it has also experienced a number of obstacles that are found in the government sector, among community members and at the GBM headquarters. The major ones are as discussed below.

In the Government

It is indeed a terrible shame that it is mainly bad governance that has led to the several blemishes that taint the image of Mother Africa today and consequently disempower many of her people. Some people believe that Africans live impoverished lives because they are unproductive and lack initiative, but nothing can be further from the truth. Much has to do with misgovernance by their leaders and Africans have been poorly governed for a long time. As a result, several obstacles have emerged that continue to hamper development activities. Some of these obstacles are addressed below.

First, because the government fails to implement many of its policies, the development and maintenance of infrastructure remain unattended to; this makes the implementation of development initiatives difficult. For instance, because of the poorly maintained roads, many regions are not easily accessible; access takes a long time and tends to damage resources (e.g. vehicles). These unnecessary losses of time and finances drag the rate and quality of development outputs.

Secondly, poor economic policies and embezzlement of funds by government officials and those connected to them also stall development, since these criminal acts affect the economy in adverse ways such as through increased living costs and unemployment. When people are living in abject poverty, they are less willing to learn about or care for their environment, especially if doing so does not directly contribute toward the fulfillment of their immediate needs. In fact, a people living in poverty and desperation will not hesitate to destroy the environment if they believe that in doing so their needs will be met.

Thirdly, some NGOs have been outspoken against the government because of its unceasing malpractice. This has led to unwillingness by the government to cooperate with such organizations—even on development issues. GBM is one such NGO whose tree-planting program in the drier regions of Kenya has remained a difficult task, since the government is slow at playing its role in providing the basic requirements for development (e.g. water projects). Government officials choose to ignore organizations such as GBM so as not to threaten their jobs, which they could easily lose if seen to be co-operating with government "enemies" (see fig. 7.1).

Lastly, though some government extension officers have played a great role in helping community members implement their activities, others have been irresponsible. They have left communities to carry out activities on their own without proper knowledge and/or techniques. Because many of these community members have little or no education, some have wasted a lot of time and resources trying to solve problems such as destruc-

Fig 7.1: *The author (second left) with opposition members of parliament, James Orengo (partly hidden to her right) and Njehu Gatabaki (in white on the author's left) being restrained by hired men in Karura Forest.*
(Photo: Courtesy of Nation Media Group)

tion of crops by white ants, moles or livestock. Others invest a lot of time and resources on their farms, only to discover that they are farming incorrect species of crops.

All these are issues that could be easily solved and avoided if the government increased its dedication and commitment to its people.

In the Community

First, although many community members now understand the importance of environmental conservation, there are still some who think that conservation is solely the duty of the government and not their own. Others think that since many people have already been mobilized to care for the environment, their help is not required. Such misunderstandings come about because the majority of the people are poorly educated and therefore do not easily make the connection between their daily problems and the environmental degradation that is the root cause of some of their problems.

Second, some communities, especially pastoralists, are difficult to work with because they are always on the move and are therefore unable to take care of seedlings. Besides, they live in areas where there is a lot of wildlife that, along with their livestock, feed on the seedlings, thus making it difficult for them to survive. No doubt they too want to conserve their environment, but, like the farming communities, they are more interested in activities that will help them meet their immediate needs. To tackle this difficulty, more financial resources are needed to fence off large areas and keep animals out until trees are mature enough to survive. And the people need to be educated to adopt new ways to co-exist sustainably with nature—especially because some of the land they once utilized for pastures has now been permanently settled by people from communities who practice farming.

Thirdly, dishonesty among some group members and also among the tree-nursery groups' support staff frustrated the progress of the tree-planting campaign. This often disappointed the other group members and resulted in the dormancy of some groups. Reactivating such dormant tree nurseries was expensive in terms of both finances and time. It also caused delays in the compilation of donor reports and made it difficult to meet project deadlines.

Another constraint has been the inability by some to perceive the long-term dangers of neglecting the environment. Although they have seen environments deteriorating elsewhere, they are still not particularly concerned, especially because their land does not seem to be undergoing degradation. However, they fail to realize that environmental degradation is gradual and that, by the time the effects are easily recognizable, it will probably be too late to implement simple and inexpensive reclamation measures.

At the Headquarters

In an attempt to curb cheating in the field, GBM gradually developed what is now known as the Ten-Step Procedure as its tree-planting methodology. Though the procedure did not stop people from trying to be dishonest, it allowed those monitoring the project to detect malpractice. Although the methodology has been criticized as being too long and tedious, especially for the rural women, it nevertheless had strengths that are largely responsible for the success that has been realized.

Tree planting in the rural areas with women's groups was an activity that attracted poor people. Consequently, the support staff for the groups both in the field and the headquarters had no training beyond secondary education. Although they performed relatively well, they lacked self-confidence, experience, exposure and commitment. For this reason, professionals undervalued them and perceived them as low-caliber staff, thereby denying them the credit that they deserved for accomplishments achieved by GBM.

In conclusion, community development remains a challenging task. It therefore requires that all stakeholders cooperate and consistently put in the effort required of them so as to eliminate the obstacles that hamper the improvement of community livelihoods.

8: LESSONS LEARNED

D uring the last twenty years of fieldwork, the Green Belt Movement has gained a lot of experience and learned many valuable lessons about community development and environmental conservation. Since other community-based projects exist and indeed more are constantly being established, the experience of GBM is recorded for the benefit of the organization and any other development stakeholders who might find this experience worthwhile.

1. COMMUNITY DEVELOPMENT INITIATIVES SHOULD ADDRESS COMMUNITY-FELT NEEDS. *(see fig. 8.1)*

Many people in developing countries are both poor and concerned about basic needs like food, water, clothing and education. Therefore, development projects must address such needs and not those that the community considers luxurious. This is why the Green Belt Movement uses tree planting as an entry-point into communities since the trees meet many felt needs of rural communities.

Fig 8.1: For women, animal fodder is a felt need.

It is necessary to conduct community needs-assessments because, first, they help to identify and prioritize the needs that given communities have. Secondly, one can use the information to identify those inter-related needs that can be addressed simultaneously through appropriate projects. Thirdly, it guides planners and motivators in the selection of development approaches that are acceptable and practical to communities.

This assessment is extremely important, because if an initiative does not address a community felt need, it is likely to grind to a halt after the initial excitement of the community members subsides.

2. THE MESSAGE MUST MAKE SENSE TO THE PARTICIPANTS.

Messages such as the protection of genetic resources, concerns over climate change and the ozone layer depletion are very important to conservationists. But how does one explain their importance to community members, the majority of whom are illiterate or semi-literate? It is necessary to deliver the conservation message in a manner that the audience will understand and appreciate.

For instance, one can ask community members to list the various ways that their families use/d the local biodiversity (e.g. as medicine, for construction, in traditional value- and spiritual-based ceremonies, as food and fodder). Such participatory discussions bring indigenous trees back into communities' daily lives and helps them to perceive the environment as a real and living part of their communal life. Yet another way is to discuss the possibility of attracting birds and other animals back to a given area, through reforestation, for the sake of current and future generations. Once such powerful but simple messages are understood, people become convinced and begin to take action.

3. THERE IS NEED FOR GOOD LEADERSHIP.

Many rural communities have experienced corruption and deceit, so much so that some now practice it as if it is the norm. Some say that it is the only development "benefit" that trickled down from the top. Corruption is especially true of those in leadership positions, since it is they who have access to community resources that they can grab to enrich themselves. Yet most stakeholders prefer an honest, fair and just system. Therefore, if a community feels that a given project is honestly run and designed to specifically benefit them, they will support and develop a strong sense of belonging to it. The less exposed a rural population is to modern lifestyles and values, the more they appreciate and expect a high sense of moral justice and fair play. It is a fact that the greatest damage done to Africa has been by the highly educated African elite, who are exposed to modern lifestyles and values and who have not adopted a culture of honesty and accountability to the people they lead. They are not role models in leadership.

4. WORK PATIENTLY TO MOTIVATE COMMUNITIES.

Working with rural communities can be very frustrating and therefore calls for much patience. Ideas, especially when they are abstract, must be simply and repeatedly presented before they are internalized. Mobilizing communities is also quite a task. GBM encouraged its members to develop a strong commitment to conservation, rather than focus only on the financial rewards. It worked gradually but mainly because GBM staff demonstrated, by example, the same commitment that they asked community members to adopt; they led patiently and by example.

5. OFFER SOME SHORT-TERM INCENTIVES.

It is important for people to see some success within a reasonable period of time. Developing both short-term and long-term objectives will create momentum for a project. When a Green Belt tree nursery is set up, for example, the first batch of tree seedlings is released to the community within three to six months. In return, the group responsible for the nursery receives compliments and appreciation from the community; this is a short-term incentive. And while members of the community are paying attention to the short-term objectives, such as supply of firewood and building materials, the long-term ones, such as soil conservation, are gradually but implicitly being realized.

6. REACH BOTH DECISION MAKERS AND COMMUNITIES AT THE SAME TIME.

Many politicians and decision makers in the developing world are the rich, the elite and the powerful. Unfortunately, many pay only lip service to the issue of conservation, since they are usually involved, directly or indirectly, in the plundering of resources. However, it is sometimes difficult to effectively take the message of conservation to the rural communities without the support of these decision makers. Even though it may take the decision makers a long time before their support is more than rhetoric, a verbal commitment to the project by the leader is essential. Rural communities become more enthusiastic about a project if their leaders are supportive.

7. FIELD STAFF MUST BE KEEN OBSERVERS.

It is important for field development workers to develop themselves into keen listeners and observers. This is because community members sometimes will make subtle but crucial comments, use body language, and even discuss issues deeply after, and not during, a meeting. Only a keen and patient development worker is able to pick up on these points and wisely bring them to the table for discussion.

8. THE COMMUNITY MUST UNDERSTAND THE PROJECT.

Some projects have such complicated and detailed designs that it is sometimes tempting to exclude certain details from the community. While this may sometimes be justifiable, it is very important for the project officials to gradually communicate these details to the community. Although this may be taxing, it must be done because as community members invest their time, they gain the capacity to clearly perceive the project in its totality, share this knowledge with others and play greater roles in the development and management of the project at the grassroots level and beyond. In addition, members will be able to assist in record keeping if they have a good understanding of the project.

Fig 8.2: *The community must own the project.*

9. THE COMMUNITY MUST OWN THE PROJECT.

GBM has spent a lot of time educating group members on the need to conserve the environment. With time, they have gradually owned the projects, especially the tree-planting campaign, since they understood it and saw its benefits. They now undertake tree planting to meet their needs rather than those of the founder (*see fig. 8.2*).

10. COMMUNITY DEVELOPMENT
TAKES COMMITMENT.

All those who have played a significant role in the development and running of GBM over the years agree that a lot of commitment is required to develop a community development project. GBM is fortunate to have had many committed employees and volunteers, some of whom continue to patiently and persistently invest a lot of time and expertise in the organization. This is undoubtedly one of the major reasons why GBM has been successful.

Additionally, the management at the headquarters has maintained a genuine concern for the people in the field. Such commitment is very crucial because it keeps the vision in focus, motivates the staff and guards against greed and the desire for personal gain; however, there have been some shortcomings. It is the lack of commitment to the target groups that has, unfortunately, led to the collapse of many organizations in Kenya that were established with promising missions. It is also worth noting that unless the upper management gains the trust of the people at the grass roots, the development process will eventually cease or remain painstakingly slow.

The community must also be committed, since they are major players in the implementation of community development projects. Unless they are dedicated, there is little progress that can be made regardless of the level of efficiency of the upper managerial staff.

Lastly, community development is often a slow process. This is because of a number of reasons, including poverty and low literacy levels among the people. Community development workers must, therefore, with patience and persistence, focus on the long term as much as they do on the short term. Failure to recognize this has led many community development workers to frustration.

11. LIMITED RESOURCES DEMAND PRIORITIZATION.

Many members of society think that GBM, having recently celebrated its twentieth anniversary, has many resources for its operations. This is certainly not so; there are a number of initiatives that GBM would like to implement for the benefit of communities, but it lacks the necessary resources. It has therefore been necessary to prioritize projects.

In addition, as a way of overcoming the constraints brought about by limited resources, it has become increasingly necessary for development initiatives to implement strategies for income generation.

12. DEMOCRATIC ADMINISTRATION AND MANAGEMENT IS KEY.

It is very important to interact with communities in a democratic manner right from the beginning of a development initiative, for a number of reasons. First, it triggers the building of trust between the secretariat and the community. Second, it emphasizes to the community that they too are project stakeholders. Third, it allows for the creation of a lasting atmosphere where views can be honestly exchanged in a participatory manner.

9 : WHY BOTHER?

Since the Green Belt Movement became known to environmentalists, especially those outside Kenya, I have been invited to many forums to give talks on it. In addressing the many issues and concerns that the Movement tackles at both the grass roots and other developmental levels, I am usually asked certain questions like "Why bother?," "What motivates you?" and "What inspires you?" The answers to these questions lie partly in my life experiences.

In responding, in both words and action, I prefer to draw upon my experiences not only within GBM but also from the various institutions of higher learning that I attended, and also from the National Council of Women of Kenya, where I spent close to twenty years as both an active member of the Executive Committee and Chairwoman (*see fig. 9.1*). I indeed also draw from my interactions with many individuals with whom, and organizations with which, I am in contact.

My life has been greatly influenced by the formal education I received during the early part of my life both at home, in Kenya, and abroad. My first four years of primary education were spent at Ihithe Primary school, located about three kilometers from our Kanungu home. The next four years of primary education were at Mathari Girls Intermediate School. My high school education

Fig 9.1: *The author (center) at a board meeting with women of NCWK "reaching out to serve." To the author's left are Eddah Gachukia, E. Karani and Priscilla Ng'endo Mereka. To the author's right are Jane Kirui and Leah Kiptanui.*

was completed at Loreto Convent Limuru Girls High School. Throughout this period, my teachers—who were mostly foreign missionaries—influenced me greatly, especially because they were positive, self-giving and value-driven.

A scholarship made available through the Catholic Bishop of Nyeri made it possible for me to join the famous Kennedy lift of the 1960s that benefited over three hundred young Kenyans. I enrolled at Mt. St. Scholastica College in Atchison, Kansas, and pursued a liberal arts education majoring in biological sciences. From Kansas, I proceeded to the University of Pittsburgh for a master's program in Biological Sciences and gained skills in tissue processing and developmental anatomy.

In 1966, I returned to Kenya and, with the assistance of Dr. Ndiritu Mathenge (the first African Dean of the Faculty of Veterinary Medicine) and the then head of the department of

Anatomy, Professor Reino Hofmann of the University of Giessen. I joined the University of Nairobi as a research assistant. I taught microanatomy until 1982, when I resigned to become involved in civic affairs.

The privilege of a higher education, especially outside Africa, broadened my horizons and was responsible for my deeper understanding of the linkages between the environment, women and development. It was this education that also helped me understand the value of working for the greater common good of communities.

I was myself a beneficiary of the common concern of others and, once successful, wanted to improve the quality of life of those I had left behind, in my country in particular, and in the African region in general. The foreign experience deepened my spirituality rather than my religion and encouraged me to seek God in myself and in others, rather than in the heavens. It gave me values worth pursuing and sharing. I set out to share those values with others through service in voluntary organizations that included the Academic Union of the University of Nairobi, the Kenya Association of University Women, the Red Cross, the League of Friends of Kenyatta Hospital, Environment Liaison Centre International, the Nyeri Women Association and the National Council of Women of Kenya.

In GBM, the importance of values is emphasized even though many people have yet to embrace the values of the organization (see Chapter Three). However, there remains a conscious effort to inculcate them in those who subscribe to the Green Belt Movement—whether in the secretariat or out in the field. These values are partly responsible not only for the original inspiration but also for the energy that sustains the organization.

It is partly as a result of all these experiences that I came to understand the linkage between environmental degradation and the felt needs of communities. This understanding was unsettling and inspired me to action. Recognizing the enormity of the problems and the need to involve as many people as possible, my friends, colleagues and I reached out to the constituency of women with which we were interacting in the National Council of Women of Kenya. In later years, it was the need for mass action that partly inspired civic and environmental education within GBM.

10: HOW TO ESTABLISH AND RUN A GREEN BELT TREE-PLANTING CAMPAIGN: THE TEN-STEP PROCEDURE

Over the years, many people have inquired about how to initiate a tree-planting campaign similar to that of the Green Belt Movement. Though it is a good question, it is by no means an easy one to answer because there exists no blueprint for GBM; rather, it achieves its objectives by formulating and revising its strategies until efficiency is achieved and outputs are attained. Because the ability to streamline and fine tune strategies comes with experience, GBM encourages those interested in establishing similar initiatives to adopt its methodology, modify it as necessary and then implement it—preferably on small scale in the initial stages.

The Ten-Step Procedure for a Potential Initiator
A detailed description of the ten-step procedure is laid out to help you, the initiator, to establish a tree-planting initiative similar to that of the Green Belt Movement.

Step 1: *Information dissemination to raise public awareness and establish contact with groups*

If you, the initiator, intend to work at the grassroots level, you may find that many people will be ignorant about issues of environmental degradation and conservation, sustainable development, tree nursery management and even tree planting. Though a few may be aware of the effects of environmental degradation (e.g. desertification, soil erosion, gullies, malnutrition, disease, etc.), you may still find them ignorant of the linkages between these effects and their causes. The reasons for this are numerous and include the belief that environmental calamities are acts of God.

Therefore, it is important to disseminate information with an aim to raise public awareness on the primary causes of environmental degradation, and on the importance and benefits of conservation. For such campaigns, messages can be spread through popular media such as newspapers, radio and television and through community meetings, seminars and workshops. One should also take advantage of community gatherings such as local administration meetings, church services and so on (*see fig. 10.1*).

Step 2: *Group Formation*

In many of the less developed countries, community members usually organize themselves into groups for development purposes. It is important for the initiator to evaluate the ability of the existing systems of organization in a community to conduct the project. It is counterproductive to ask people to form new groups if they have already established other more effective and sustainable ways of organizing themselves. The advantage of working with groups is that a large section of the community (or stakeholders) is mobilized. In addition, such a project stands a greater

Fig 10.1: Step Two: Disseminating information to interested members of the public.

chance of success when its operations do not heavily rely on a small minority. If it becomes essential to form groups, it is important to allow them to form freely—without coercion—since that is essential for the cohesion and dynamics of groups. When forming groups, members are encouraged to elect their leaders through secret ballot to encourage democratic decision making. If they do not already have a bank account, they are encouraged to establish one and identify signatories since GBM normally pays groups through checks.

To assist them to focus and also operate efficiently, it is very important to provide group members with enough information about the nature of the project at this stage. This includes the goals of the project, methodology, inputs, risks, expected short- and long-term outputs, and benefits. For the establishment of tree nurseries, groups need to be informed of the preparatory work, which includes searching for seeds and cuttings, transplanting seedlings, supervising work at the nursery site, record-keeping and carrying out follow-ups.

Providing people with information during group formation avoids misunderstandings that could arise as a result of ignorance on the part of group members or because of greed. The initiator should consider drawing up a constitution, or simply laying down a set of rules to be agreed on and to guide all stakeholders.

Language is also important. GBM prefers to use the language that most stakeholders understand. Unless there are restrictions, it is recommended that the initiator adopt the same trend. If the groups still need assistance with communication (e.g. filling out forms), community leaders such as schoolteachers can be very helpful, and indeed they have been helpful in GBM for many years.

Step 3: Locating a tree-nursery site and registration of tree-nursery groups

Once a group is formed, the members look for an appropriate piece of land to establish their green belt. If they decide to use public land and find themselves in need of assistance, encourage them to seek advice from the local administrators and other leaders, such as councilors, chiefs and community development officers. GBM prefers to set up nurseries on public land because that way, all members are free to visit the nursery and work on it.

Step 4: Physical establishment of a tree nursery

Preparing the nursery site includes digging trenches, making terraces, laying seedbeds and building fences. Though groups are able to do much of this work on their own, it is always good to solicit the help of resource persons such as foresters, agricultural extension officers or experienced members of GBM in neighboring areas. It is very important for groups to learn how to prepare and manage their tree nurseries properly because this determines the success of the entire project.

Without unnecessarily burdening group members with complex procedures and details, these resource persons should teach basic tree-nursery techniques that group members can quickly adopt and practice. For the benefit of conservation of local biological diversity, tree-nursery groups should be encouraged to grow indigenous trees. However, experience has shown that groups will grow seedlings that meet the felt needs of communities even when such seedlings are not appropriate for conservation of local biological diversity. Therefore, it is important to remind the groups and the community at large that conservation is important for the benefit of long-term community goals, including those of future generations.

The nurseries receive plastic bags into which to transplant the seedlings. However, because resources are often limited, methods of improvisation need to be shared with the groups at this stage. For instance, many GBM group members refrain from throwing out suitable polythene bags, tins and other containers from their homes and instead transplant seedlings into them. This keeps the nursery operational and also helps recycle some of the household "trash."

Step 5: Reporting on the progress of the nursery

GBM requires that all groups send in progress reports on a monthly basis. For this reason, each nursery is required to have a tree- nursery attendant to help women to collect data and compile reports. In these reports, the groups indicate the number and types of seedlings (indigenous, exotic or fruit) that are in the nursery, the number that are ready to be issued to members of the public and any obstacles that they face at the nursery. Such communications are essential because they maintain the link between the groups and headquarters and inform those at the headquarters on the progress being made by the groups.

Step 6: Promotion of tree planting to the community and digging of holes

When tree-nursery groups have sufficient seedlings that are ready for issue to the public, they make announcements in public gatherings such as church services and schools, in barazas (or local administration meetings) and also through house visits; this exercise is called promotion.

During promotion, the tree-nursery group members request those interested in planting trees to dig holes with diameters and depths of about two feet. After the holes are inspected and approved by a member of a given tree nursery, the seedlings are issued. Community members willing to plant trees but unaware of what GBM recommends are instructed by the mini-advisor, nursery attendant or any group member. The instructions include basic techniques like ensuring that seedlings are removed from plastic containers before planting, containers are recycled and manure is applied to the holes where soils are poor.

Step 7: Establishment of public and private green belts

GBM defines a "green belt" as a woodlot established by planting several trees on a piece of land that can either be public or private. To establish a public green belt, one should aim at planting at least one thousand trees, while a private one should aim for at least one hundred trees. The reason for giving these targets was to encourage the groups to plant trees in large numbers. However, some public and private green belts have been established with fewer trees, while others have thousands more.

Public Green Belts

Any public institution that wishes to join the organization can contact any local tree nursery group or GBM field-staff member for details on the procedure.

Those involved in the establishment of green belts are encouraged to form an elected green belt committee to oversee it and to identify a community member, preferably handicapped, to help nurture it; this person is known as a Green Belt Ranger. GBM supports the green belt by providing garden tools and water tanks as a token of appreciation and incentive. These tools are initially used by the ranger but eventually become the property of the public institution. When green belts are established on school compounds, teachers are encouraged to fully involve students in the planting and nurturing processes.

Private Green Belts

Any individual who wishes to establish a private green belt is also requested to contact the local tree-nursery group or field staff in the area for details. Seedlings are issued, free of charge, only after a group member has confirmed that holes have been dug. GBM does not provide tools to facilitate a private green belt since the organization prefers to work with the larger community as opposed to individuals.

In the past, GBM provided seedlings, at no charge, for the establishment of both public and private green belts. Recently, however, it was suggested that GBM encourage the women's groups to sell their seedlings directly to community members as a way of generating income to sustain their nurseries and avoid dependency on the organization. Those who have received free seedlings from GBM nurseries have generally been appreciative of the work of the women and the organization. While recognizing the need for the women to commercialize their tree nurseries, GBM remains apprehensive of the ability of poor rural communities to purchase seedlings from the groups and maintain the tree-planting campaign at the same level and quality of performance.

Step 8: Planting trees and follow-up

During the rainy seasons, farmers flock to the tree-nursery sites to collect seedlings for planting. The group members then do follow-up on the seedlings twice after they are planted. The first follow-up is done after one month, and the second and final one is done after three months. This follow-up exercise is conducted to check on how the seedlings are progressing and to collect data for office records.

Step 9: First follow-up for seedlings

The objective of the first follow-up is to ensure that the seedlings that were issued were indeed planted and that this was properly done. This must be done as soon as possible—even within days—but not later than one month after planting. Promoters as well as group members are encouraged to follow up their seedlings for up to three months before the first payment is recommended by the monitor.

Step 10: Second follow-up and payment of groups

The second follow-up was given a minimum of six months to ensure that the seedlings were established and therefore likely to survive. Information gathered in the course of follow-up is forwarded to the headquarters through forms that are used for monitoring the tree-planting campaign. At the headquarters the forms are checked by monitors who, if satisfied with the information provided, approve GBM's purchase of the seedlings through payment by checks to the concerned groups and support staff. GBM pays the groups for only those seedlings that are surviving at the time of the second follow-up because these plants are not as vulnerable and can therefore survive with little or no attention.

11: THE REPLICATION OF THE GREEN BELT MOVEMENT

Since several parts of Africa face the same types of problems and challenges, similar strategies are quite often used to solve them. Having already recognized this, Dr. Mostafa Tolba, who at the time was the Executive Director of the United Nations Environment Programme (UNEP), challenged the Green Belt Movement to share its methodologies and experience with development workers, environmentalists and other stakeholders in Africa and other regions. This was during the United Nations World Conference on Women held in Nairobi in 1985.

Perceiving this as an important initiative, GBM took up the challenge and prepared a proposal that outlined the strategies through which the organization's experience could be shared. After the proposal was approved by UNEP, four workshops were held between 1986 and 1988 in which forty-five (45) participants from fifteen (15) sub-Saharan countries were trained. Unfortunately, UNEP was unable to provide funds for follow-up.

After the workshops, therefore, the Green Belt Movement immediately initiated efforts to raise more money for seed funding to implement and monitor the project that the participants had established. However, this proved difficult. One reason for this difficulty was that GBM's successful advocacy for the conservation of Uhuru Park disappointed a number of highly placed government officials who had high stakes in the park's "development." To vent their anger, these officials resorted to acts of harassment and misrepresentation toward the organization. This scared some of the participants, who felt that they would be placing themselves at risk by continuing to communicate with the organization through progress reports and public affiliation. This fear was justified because their own governments were still rather oppressive, under one political party, and plagued with the Big Man of Africa syndrome, which resisted grassroots initiatives—especially those that tended to unite and organize people. Without progress reports, it was difficult to raise any funds. This disenabling political environment also made it difficult for staff from GBM to travel to these countries to evaluate participants' projects. Again, without evaluation reports, fund-raising efforts were frustrated.

Since it proved difficult for the staff of GBM to travel to these countries, it became necessary to reunite the participants in Nairobi to discuss their progress. A reunion was therefore held in 1992. During these discussions, participants shared what they had experienced in their countries. From these discussions the conclusion was drawn that, with commitment and financial support, it was possible to replicate the Green Belt Movement approach. The Green Belt Movement noted this conclusion and, as a result, the Pan-African Green Network was formed at that reunion. This network was meant to assist groups and individuals to initiate Green Belt activities or incorporate aspects of its approach in their own ongoing activities. During the reunion, participants also recommended that additional workshops be held for those in African countries who had not yet participated, and for members of tree- nursery groups within the network.

Therefore, in 1993, a fourth workshop was organized for another group of participants, especially from countries that had not yet participated. However, raising funds continued to prove difficult. Consequently, many participants lost both interest and contact.

It was not until 1998 that the next Pan-African workshop was organized. This was with the financial support of Comic Relief of Great Britain, popularized as the Red Nose Appeal and now known as Charity Projects. It provided a grant to revisit the initiative and intensify its efforts.

During the first four workshops, much experience was gained that helped in the development of a more effective training project. The current mode of operation of this project is as follows:

Selection of Candidates

Rather than post a general advertisement and have individuals apply directly to GBM, the participants are selected through well-established environmental organizations in the target countries. Directors of these organizations are requested to recommend the candidates and commit their organizations to support them after the training. This process increases the chances of getting pro-active and committed participants. Both the directors and the prospective participants are required to fill out forms and questionnaires that are processed by GBM according to the criteria of the project. After the selection is complete, travel and accommodation arrangements are made for the participants.

To encourage women to attend, the training program has been shortened from four to two weeks. This is because women are unable to stay away from home for too long a period, considering their domestic responsibilities. In addition, GBM ensures that a gender balance is maintained when selecting participants.

The Training Program

The overall goal of the program is to raise the consciousness of the participants so that they come to appreciate and actively care for the environment. The training workshops last for two weeks, and in that time all costs, including those of the participants, are met using funds from Comic Relief, the sole funding agent of this project at this time (1998–2001). During the workshop, the participants:

- Gain exposure to the various environmental problems that exist in Kenya
- Carry out comparative discussions on the problems in Kenya and those in their respective countries
- Improve their abilities to conceptualize ideas and solutions to problems
- Learn how to formulate, implement and evaluate action plans
- Learn how action plans are used in development initiatives
- Pay a visit to the field to hold discussions and practical demonstrations with GBM women's groups on the organization's approach to environmental conservation
- Discuss other GBM projects in an effort to address issues such as project sustainability
- Learn how to write proposals, monitor and evaluate projects, manage finances and establish good donor relations
- Write their proposals
- Present proposals to a select committee

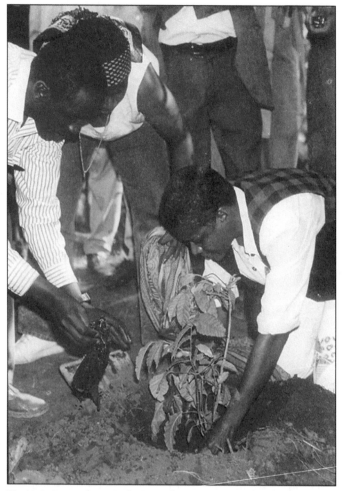

Fig 11.1: A participant at the Pan-African Green Network plants a tree at the completion of the workshop. Assisting is Gathuru Mbura (front left).

Although the original aim of these workshops was to have participants replicate the Green Belt Movement in their own countries, it quickly became clear that this was not practical, because not all of the organizations from which participants came had visions and missions that were similar to GBM's. To avoid possible conflicts of interest, the organization recently agreed to encourage participants to promote green consciousness in their organizations and use the GBM approach only in areas where it is effective.

After the committee approves the presented proposals, it presents certificates of participation to all candidates and also invites them to become members of the Pan-African Green Network. At this stage, they have acquired enough information to enable them to effectively tackle various environmental problems. After returning to their respective countries, participants are given time to satisfactorily fulfill a number of criteria after which GBM provides seed funding for them to begin the project implementation.

Three workshops were held, in 1988, 1999 and 2000, with 50 participants attending.

The interest in replicating the Green Belt approach has also been demonstrated by people from outside Africa. These include students of women's studies, rural development and/or African affairs who wish to study the organization or gain experience in the field as interns. Environmentally conscious groups wishing to initiate similar activities to those of GBM in urban neighborhoods have also expressed interest.

One such environmentally conscious group is comprised of the Board members of the Jane Addams Conference in Leadership, an organization based in Chicago, Illinois. Members of this organization have in the past encouraged the development of green belts in Chicago's poor neighborhoods. Another interested group is from Haiti. The Haiti initiative was inspired by the then Vice-President of the United States of America, Al Gore, who expressed concern over the environmental deterioration in Haiti. In 1995, he asked the Green Belt Movement to assist Haitian groups to replicate the Green Belt approach in Haiti's degraded hillsides so as to reclaim them. However, this project was frustrated by lack of funds.

It was not until the year 2000 that this was overcome by the efforts of GROOTS International, an organization led by a group of women from New York, where GROOTS is based. These women included Peggy Snyder, Caroline Pezzulo and Lisel Burns. They managed to raise enough funds to send two women to the training workshop that GBM held in September 2000. GROOTS has also taken up the responsibility of monitoring the initiatives that will be implemented in Haiti.

It is the environmental values that are based on many aspects of human endeavor that will change the environmental map of Africa. That change must come from within. At the end of the workshop of November 1999, Litha Sovell of Tanzania beautifully captured this conviction and spirit in the following poem, which she composed for the closing ceremony:

Now We Are Green, Our Touch Is Green

We came from East, red as we are
We came from West, white as we are
We came from South, black as we are
Now we are green, our touch is green.

Now we know, green is something
Now we know, seeds are valuable
Now we know, seeds are trees
Now we are green, our touch is green.

Soil is life, we know of it

Soil is wealth, we have a lot of it
Soil is gold, we keep it forever
Now we are green, our touch is green.

Now we know, grabbing land is evil
Now we know, land is for all
Now we know, land is prestige
Now we are green, our touch is green.

Now we know, we are all brothers
Now we know, we are all sisters
Now we know, we share the earth
Now we know, our touch is green.

Thanks for coming, now we are going
Thanks for seeds, which are patent-free
Now we can plant our seeds all over
Now we are green, our touch is green.

Now we are leaders, we lead our people
Now we are people, people of action
Now we are planters, we tell the people
Now we are green, our touch is green.

Let us unite, speak the same
Let us unite, tell we are living
Let us unite, enjoy our wealth
Now we are green, our touch is green.
We didn't know Kenya, Tanzania are ours
We didn't know Ghana, Uganda are ours
We didn't know Zimbabwe, Ethiopia are ours

Now we know our touch is green.

Goodbye we say, we know it is not over
We wish to stay, but our people need us
We are in a hurry, seedlings are ready
Now we are green, our touch is green.

Litha Sovell
GBM-Tanzania
November 1998

12: THE WAY FORWARD

At various periods in the past twenty years of GBM work, a number of evaluations have been conducted, including those sponsored by CARE-Austria (1996) and NOVIB of the Netherlands (1997). The CARE and NOVIB evaluations were important particularly because they closely examined the sustainability of GBM with respect to tree planting, income generation, geographical spread and institutional strength.

Major conclusions drawn from these evaluations were that if it did not change its strategies, GBM and its constituency would become too dependent on donor funds for its work—clearly an unsustainable development approach. Consequently, it was recommended and accepted that GBM would undertake an Organizational Development (OD) process through which it would reassess and reflect on its past and vision, and develop a new strategic plan.

On completion of the OD process, the new vision and mission of GBM were as follows:

THE VISION

To create a society of people who consciously work for continued improvement of their livelihoods and a greener, cleaner Kenya.

The key elements in this vision are that people must first understand and internalize the linkage between environmental degradation and unsustainable livelihoods so as to make conscious efforts—driven by strong felt needs and convictions—to improve their livelihoods through environmental conservation.

THE MISSION

To mobilize community consciousness for self-determination, equity, improved livelihood securities and environmental conservation using trees as the entry point.

In the mission, there are two key elements; first, environmental conservation must go hand in hand with poverty eradication. Secondly, people must be helped to understand their status and that of their surroundings, and then empowered to take responsibility for their own destiny—rather than wait for others to do the determination.

GBM Programs

To realize its mission and vision, GBM incorporated both core and institutional strengthening programs into its strategic plan. These are listed and discussed below:

The Core Programs

- Tree planting on public lands

- Food security at the household level
- Civic and environmental education
- Networking and advocacy

The Institution-Strengthening Programs
- Business development
- Capacity building

Tree Planting on Public Lands Program
Objective

To inculcate in local communities a culture of planting indigenous trees on public lands as a means for beautifying the countryside, reclaiming denuded areas and preventing further environmental degradation.

Approach

GBM will shift from tree planting on private lands and focus on public land in its tree-planting campaign.

These public lands include:
a) Institutional grounds (e.g. hospital grounds, school grounds, church grounds, chiefs' camps)
b) Statutory reserves (e.g. riverbanks, roadsides, wells, marshes, hills, mountain buffer zones, water catchments)
c) Urban centers
d) Environmental degradation hot spots (e.g. denuded steep slopes, gullies, rocky places, dry riverbeds)
e) Sites of cultural significance

Communities will be encouraged to plant indigenous trees and long-lasting fruit trees because these have characteristics such as well-spread root systems, thick trunks, widespread branches, foliage and good shade. These characteristics favor air purification, prevention of over-evaporation of moisture from the soil, and anchorage and enrichment of soil by root systems and falling leaves. These factors make indigenous trees superior to exotic ones.

In the course of promoting indigenous trees on public lands, groups will also be encouraged to raise seedlings of fruit trees, some of which will be sold in the markets to the surrounding communities, while others will be planted on the farms of group members. This promotional activity will simply be a by-product of the core program of planting trees on public lands.

While in Phase I groups received compensation for the seedlings that they issued, Phase II will focus on the commercialization of the tree nurseries by the women themselves. The demand exists because many farmers have experienced the benefits of tree planting on their farms. However, groups will need to proactively promote their seedlings to the farmers in a real business sense.

As a starting point for the Phase II tree-planting program, all groups in a given sub-location will together form a sub-location green network. The role of the network will primarily be twofold: first, to promote ideals of environmental conservation, and second, to plant trees on public lands. The networks will be provided with basic training especially in relation to the collection of seeds and raising of seedlings for indigenous trees.

It is recognized that certain species of indigenous trees may be available in one region and not in another because of indiscriminate felling of trees. For such situations, GBM will organize inter-regional exchange visits where people can exchange seeds and seedlings. The result will be a wide distribution of indigenous tree diversity across the country.

In this program, as in all the others, GBM will synergize with other organizations for increased effectiveness.

Food Security at the Household Level
Objective
To assist communities in analyzing and understanding their food security risks and then learning and practicing simple, ecologically friendly initiatives that will enable them to consistently provide enough farm-sourced food, of the right quality and variety, for the household.

Approach
Today, there are still many households that do not have sufficient supplies of food throughout the year. In others, unbalanced diets are consumed very frequently and this has led to malnutrition—especially among children and the aged. These two occurrences are caused by a number of factors, including:

i)   Over-commercialization of agriculture, which has resulted in excessive monocropping in various areas, e.g. Transnzoia District, where maize is the dominant crop.

ii) Reduction in farm size due to overpopulation. This is true in areas such as the central highlands, where farmers, using only rudimentary farming techniques, cannot grow enough food to feed their households.

iii) Heavy reliance on cash crops though farm size is small. Some farmers depend upon cash crops to generate income to purchase food for the household. When

Fig 12.1: Arrowroots are some of the indigenous crops being promoted.

income from the cash crops is low, households are left with little or no funds to purchase food.

iv) Low productivity of the land. This is true of areas, such as Machakos, that are highly populated but yet fall into the category of marginal (or low-productivity) lands. In these areas, it is difficult to produce enough food.

The program will tackle the problem of food insecurity by enhancing the knowledge and skills of farmers on productivity improvement, indigenous crops, traditional dietary principles and variety cropping. Some of the crops and techniques to be promoted are as follows:

- Root crops: Cassava, yams, groundnuts, sweet potatoes, indigenous and exotic arrowroots (see fig. 12.1)
- Legumes: Pigeon peas, black beans, butter beans, climbing beans

- Cereals: Indigenous maize, millet, sorghum, simsim
- Tree crops: Sugar cane, bananas, indigenous fruit trees

Techniques
Composting, terracing, mulching, double-dug beds, deep digging, cut-off drains, cover cropping, simple food processing, proper storage techniques, beekeeping, seed preservation.

Activities
The food security program will be implemented as follows:

- Conduct food-security awareness meetings at each sub-location
- Help groups to identify the best farming practice
- Provide intensive food security training to best practice farmers
- Conduct inter-regional exchange visits and food festivals
- Develop a demonstration center for food security technologies at the GBM training institute
- Conduct periodic impact assessment

Grassroots Civic and Environmental Education Program
Objective
To raise awareness of primary environmental care and enhance knowledge, attitudes and values that support sustainable grassroots socio-economic and ecological welfare.

Approach
Civic and environmental education is a people's education scheme. It is education toward being a responsible citizen in all

matters affecting individual and communal livelihood. The main subject blocks of this program are:

- Environmental conservation
- Basic human rights
- Knowing one's roots (culture)
- Good governance
- GBM values
- Issues of equity
- The value of our natural resource base
- Our responsibility today towards future generations

Activities

The activities through which the objective will be achieved are as follows:

- Conduct grassroots civic and environmental education seminars
- Conduct a regular radio program on civic education
- Produce a grassroots civic education leaflet
- Initiate cultural exchange
- Produce audio cassettes of civic education lectures
- Develop local civic education units
- Conduct a school environmental education project
- Conduct periodic impact assessment

Though this program involves a number of activities, it will primarily be executed through seminars.

Advocacy and Networking Program
Objective

To bring to the national and international limelight actions of poor governance and/or abuse to the environment and then rally people's resistance to such actions.

Sometimes advocacy is viewed as militancy against governments. However, it must be recognized that many environmental problems are a result of deliberate abuse and a lack of emphasis and commitment to environmental conservation. In many cases, the illegal allotment of forests, parks and recreational spaces is done by those in high places of authority; therefore, attempts by the public to reclaim these commons are met with violence. For these reasons, environmental conservation must sometimes be effected through advocacy. To further strengthen the impact of advocacy, support from the international community is necessary, because it provides loans and grants to help manage the environment sustainably.

Approach

In the past, advocacy has been conducted through protests and mass action, which have been brought to the limelight by the print and broadcast media. These protests have been against incidents of illegal allotment of land, forest excision for private development, construction of commercial complexes in public parks, etc. In Phase II, these means of advocacy will be retained, though other advocacy activities will be incorporated, e.g. preservation of rare indigenous trees and sites of cultural significance, networking of Pan-African participants, communication with international supporters through Internet facilities, etc.

Activities

The objective of this program will be achieved through the following strategies.

- Conduct Pan-African Green Belt Movement workshops to raise green consciousness in Africa
- Provide support to participants in the Pan-African Green Belt Movement workshops to enable them to raise green consciousness in their countries
- Organize mass action events against illegal allotment of land, misuse of the environment, etc
- Produce and disseminate information on key advocacy issues
- Conduct advocacy for preservation of sites of cultural significance and rare indigenous species
- Conduct workshops for NGOs and other development agencies to promote the principles of the Earth Charter

Business Development Program

Objective

The primary focus of this program is to generate income for GBM that will be used to, at least, cover the operating expenses of the organization, or to move toward partial sustainability.

Approach

The business ideas to be pursued center on forming the GBM Institute into a training and retreat center, and developing eco-tourism, business networks and local fund-raising. At present, GBM is making substantial gain from the Lang'ata facility and eco-tourism. With a more professional approach, it seems possible that an increase in income can be realized. Of more potential is the possibility of local fund-raising, which needs to be developed from its initial stages.

Activities

The objective of this program will be achieved through the following activities:

- Develop a business plan for the GBM Institute
- Provide core funds for business plan implementation
- Hire a business manager to implement the business plan
- Conduct capacity building for staff members to run the GBM projects after three years

Capacity-Building Program

Objective

To improve the efficiency, effectiveness and image of the organization.

Approach

In the 1995 and 1997 evaluations, certain factors concerning the institutional set-up of GBM were identified as needing attention so as to improve efficiency and effectiveness. These included improvement of information storage and retrieval, financial management and reporting, research and documentation.

These and other issues will be addressed on a progressive basis over the next three years with the assistance of experts from the respective fields. Especially crucial in this area is the issue of succession planning and management strengthening through new appointments. GBM staff should have strong capabilities and potential in leadership, management, fund-raising and public relations. At the same time, the Board of Directors needs to be strengthened. Such a Board will have the custodial role for GBM policies, values, forward planning and development. Also there is the need for a grassroots consultative forum that would take the responsibilities of feeding the custodial Board with grassroots program experiences and facilitating monitoring and evaluations in the field.

Activities

These are as follows:

- Rationalize the organization structure, staff positions and remuneration
- Establish offices of new senior officers
- Computerize GBM's information and financial systems
- Provide adequate transport facilities for field monitoring
- Establish a public relations, research and documentation office
- Institutionalize office of the accountant
- Upgrade employees' skills
- Conduct public relations program to improve the image of GBM

Target Groups

As in the past, GBM will continue to work with women's groups in Phase II for the following reasons:

i)   These groups exist in every part of the country
ii) They have been exposed to the tree-planting campaign

iii) They are legally constituted

iv) In the rural set-up, food availability in the household is usually the woman's responsibility. Hence, women are the strategic target group for the food security program

In addition to these groups, other social groups, like self-help and youth groups, will also be allowed to join GBM. However, the groups in urban areas will primarily focus on urban tree planting, civic education and advocacy.

Since the strategic plan was developed through a participatory process, it is expected that with proper implementation, this rebirth of GBM will result in an even stronger organization.

AFTERWORD: AN INTERVIEW
WITH WANGARI MAATHAI

*I*n November 2003, the Worldwatch Institute's staff researcher
Danielle Nierenberg and senior fellow Mia MacDonald met in
Nairobi with Wangari Maathai. In January 2003, Maathai
became Assistant Minister for Environment, Natural Resources and
Wildlife. She was elected to Kenya's Parliament with 98% of the
vote in the country's first free and fair election in decades. Maathai,
jailed, harassed and vilified by the autocratic regime of former President Daniel arap Moi, had recently been named an "Elder of the
Burning Spear" for services to Kenya by President Mwai Kibaki.
Nierenberg and MacDonald spoke with Maathai about her transi-
tion from NGO leader and vocal government critic to minister,
Kenya's ecological challenges and what's being done to address
them, and the role of gender in her life and work.

**WW: What's it like going from being the founder of an
NGO and a prominent government critic to being part of
the government itself?**

Initially, I was not very keen on even getting into Parliament. But
I eventually felt that after so many years of work outside the government, of producing results but not enough to change the government, to try and change it from the inside. People were very,

very happy that I was elected and they were very happy that I was put in the government, but what they don't quite appreciate is if you're not the minister there are so many things you can't do because you are now working under another person. But because I have such a high prominence on the environment, people expect me to make decisions. They expect to see major evidence of revolution, because they're so concerned about what's going to happen and they want to turn things over—and they expect me to turn things over. Part of the frustration is that I know what the ministry should do. But I can't say it. The minister has to buy that idea, and do it and say it. I try to be persuasive, but [things are] not moving as fast as I would have liked.

WW: What does your being in government means for environmental activists around the world?

Many of the environmentalists with whom we started in the 1960s and 1970s did end up in government, and a good number of them became ministers. Sometimes when I'm frustrated I remember [José] Lutzenberger, in Brazil. He was minister for the environment and we were all very excited about that. Then he felt so tied up that he resigned. For many of us, because we are driven by idealism rather than politics, we have to train ourselves to be patient and realize that governments are not run by idealists. For those of us who come from that perspective you have to be patient and know that we're not going to change the big landscape; perhaps we can change the landscape of a forest.

WW: Are you hopeful about the possibilities for change?

I'm always hopeful. I'm very happy to be in this government because it's committed to change. We have opportunities to make change happen, make things take a different direction. I'm very excited, actually. Sometimes when I go into Parliament I reflect that to be in this house is a very big privilege—one of the very few that have had that opportunity in a country of 30 million people. There are 222 of us, and there are 16 or 17 women. It's a great privilege to be entrusted by the people to shape their lives through the formulation of legislation. It's [also] a very great responsibility. I try to remind myself of the responsibility and not take it for granted.

The good thing about this government is that it was voted [in] for change. So you feel that whatever you're doing, you're trying to improve on what was there before. One of the major challenges, though, is that we inherited a very mismanaged system — a system that had been riddled with so much corruption and looting of public resources. People are expecting a lot of things to be done, but we don't have the resources. We are still very indebted and dependent on the International Monetary Fund (IMF) and World Bank and other governments. That becomes a challenge because we know what we want to do, but we don't have the resources to do it.

WW: What initiatives are you working on now?
I wanted to start a national tree-planting day, and I thought that Easter would be a wonderful time. It's a long weekend with very little happening. Kenya is almost 85% Christian. And I thought because people here are crazy about religion and Jesus and crucifixion, and to get the cross, somebody has to go into the forest, cut a tree and chop it up. So there would be nothing better for the Christians to do than to plant a tree and bring back a life, like Christ came back to life. If everybody replaced the tree that was cut, you can imagine how many trees you could plant. It would be fun. We could do it every year. I wanted it announced and it

was not announced, and I was very disappointed. The minister said there was no rain. It's true; there was a dry spell. But on Easter Sunday and Easter Monday it rained cats and dogs and I said, "Well, look at this."

One of the campaigns I'm doing at the moment is trying to stop the overproduction of thin plastic, which is being thrown everywhere and is such a nuisance. We are talking to companies, and companies are being asked to stop producing them [thin plastic] and produce thicker plastic that can be recycled.

WW: What are the most important lessons from your work with GBM that you can apply to your work in government?

One of the most wonderful things we did in the GBM process was to make ordinary people become seedling producers, what we call "foresters without diploma." For many years our main thing was to try to make people understand the linkage between good governance and conservation—how a an environment that is well managed helps to sustain a good quality of life. It was easy to say, "What are your problems?" "Well, our problems are many: We have poverty. We suffer from many diseases, from malnutrition. We are hungry. We don't get paid for our produce. We are unable to educate our children. We are unable to provide ourselves with good health care. We don't have water." And then we would ask them, "Where do you think these problems come from?" Almost without doubt they would blame the government. But it was necessary for them to understand that the government is not the only culprit.

You also play a part. You do not demand a better government. You do not stand up for what you strongly believe and tell your government to provide that. Also, you have land but you're not protecting that. You're allowing soil erosion to take place and you could do something about it. You are hungry, but you are not growing food. You have opted for exotic food crops that don't grow very well in your soil and may not even be very nutritious. So you need to do something. You may not be able to do much about the government, but you can do something about what is in your power. That is what produced the tree planting campaign. And a collective responsibility gradually developed towards the management of the environment. We created a movement that was not only taking action to save the environment, but also about the responsibility we have to have as citizens, to change the government and to demand better governance.

WW: Is any of your work in the Ministry linked to GBM now?
I'm working with the Green Belt Movement to continue producing seedlings in their thousands. I'm waiting for the ministry to be able to say we can buy these seedlings. If we said we can buy these seedlings, we would get them in the millions. That would be wonderful: you'd put a lot of people to work in the rural areas. When they [the seedlings] are ready, the government could go and collect [them] and pay the women. You don't have to pay them much—five shillings—not even 10 U.S. cents. You're putting money into the hands of very poor people and they are working for it.

Next Friday we'll be planting trees in Aberdare Forest [near Mount Kenya]. Green Belt people have produced the seedlings and I persuaded the forester to allow them to come into the forest and plant their trees. The forester is very happy because he doesn't have trees and he needs them. So there is a partnership between the people and the forester, and the provincial administration is also participating. I'm trying to do there what I'd like to see replicated in the country. I'm doing it in my constituency so nobody can tell me, "What are you doing?"

WW: What are the main challenges Kenya's environment faces?

Deforestation—how to recover forest cover—how to save our wildlife, how to give ourselves adequate water and how to curb pollution. Because of the work we did [in GBM] there is a lot of concern over the forests. Forest cover has been reduced very quickly, to about 1.7%, and the level recommended by the UN Environment Program (UNEP) is about 10% at the very minimum. Two-thirds of our country is arid, semi-arid, and desert. We are very vulnerable with the Sahara Desert right here and we are an agricultural country. So we need to increase forest cover, and the only way you can do it, really, is by involving the people.

WW: Do you think reforestation is possible, despite population and development pressures?

It is doable. We have a high population pressure, but we tend to congregate in one-third of our country, where we have water and good soil and mountains—forested mountains. But two-thirds is out there and should be utilized more. I've been advocating for afforestation in those areas with exotic species of trees that grow fast and are commercially very exploitable and for many years have been planted on the mountains. I'm suggesting we should plant fewer of those exotic trees in the mountains and more indigenous trees there because we also want to protect the catchment areas and the diversity of the plants and the animals.

WW: You want to make it economically viable, too, right?
Exotic species can do very well in dry areas. But this is also something that will require some thinking and convincing, because for the last 80 years or so we have been planting exotic species for the timber industry, mostly in the indigenous forests. We have literally been cutting indigenous forests to replace them with exotics. That's what we were fighting [in GBM]. Now I'm trying to convince others that we need to reverse that, but the thinking is kind of fixed. So it will take some convincing. Slowly, I am convinced, they will see sense in taking plantations of exotic species in other areas, so they are grown as a crop. These [indigenous] forests? Don't even think about them. Forget them. Don't go there harvesting.

WW: What are some of the obstacles?
One of the major challenges to overcome the issue of deforestation is to involve people, as many people as possible in production of seedlings and planting [them]. The public is ready for that kind of engagement. In fact, members of Parliament are ready. I'm asked by members of Parliament constantly to help them establish tree nurseries in their area, to go and speak to their women, to have them establish tree nurseries. The political will is there. So, the opportunity is great, and the good thing is that GBM is there, too.

WW: What about corruption in the forestry sector, which was a focus of your work with GBM, stopping the "land grabbing," the forest excisions, etc.?
Right now we have sent all foresters home because so many were corrupt and they were destroying the forest. As we speak, they are being re-interviewed to see whom we shall keep and whom

we shall let go. This was really a drastic action, getting rid of all of them and having to re-interview them and assess them and re-employ them if they can be and send them away and do another re-employment. We still have a lot of challenges in how we are going to be able to manage our forests. Involving the public is very important, because the public has been persuaded to perceive the forest as being the property of the government—it's none of their business. So, these foresters with their corruption were able to go in there and destroy forests while the public watched. The public didn't raise the alarm and it was left to a few organizations like us. But the more people get involved, the more we can fight corruption at the local level. To me this is the biggest fight against corruption as far as the forests are concerned.

WW: How is the fight against forest corruption and destruction different now than when you were part of the NGO community?
When we were in the Green Belt Movement, we were civil society pointing fingers at the people we thought were corrupt, at the government for not being able to do something about it. Now that we're in the government, one of the good things is that the president and the entire government is very committed to fighting corruption. It has been one of our major concerns in this country and we have done a lot of things that point to the culprit. We want to eliminate the problem although it's not going to be an overnight thing. It's so entrenched.

WW: How do you deal with the expectations of you now that you're in government, given the high profile you have had in Kenya for so many years?
One of the complaints people have is that they were so used to

hearing my voice all the time and now they don't hear my voice. I'm telling them, "when you're in the government you cannot complain because you can't complain to yourself. You're part of the system now. So to whom do I complain? I can only try to change from within."

They also see me as an action-oriented person. They want to see action; they don't want to hear that I'm sitting there when the forests are disappearing. The challenge for me is to be able to do things that they can see without being overbearing, because I am only in the assistant minister position.

WW: Do you feel pressure?

Yes, it gives me a sense of pressure—that I must produce a result; that I must demonstrate that the government is not asleep, but we are indeed there to do the work, that we are actually delivering. That's part of the reason why I'm trying to say, "well, let's declare this national tree planting day," and I'm saying "now let's go and tell people to plant seedlings." For me, seedling production is like kid stuff. I've done it for the last quarter century. I know it can be done and it doesn't overwhelm me because I know it can be done. If we did it, it would be the first time that the government is working directly with the community to try to rehabilitate the environment. In the past, the government was operating completely separate from the civil society and the communities.

WW: But you're not thinking "government is not for me"?

No, no, no, no, no. I believe this for me the next step and it is a very, very important step. For me it's learning. I'm learning that things don't work as easily as that, that there are so many issues that need to be considered. But it is also important for one to think that if you are going to deliver, if you are going to make the

changes that the people are looking for, that you can't afford to
move so slowly. One of the exciting aspects is being able to make
laws. I sit there in Parliament sometimes and remind myself,
"You're really making laws here." If you can help make laws that
will make things better tomorrow then that's much, much better
than what you could have done outside. If a law is made then you
actually have an opportunity to influence future generations.

**WW: What's been the impact of your gender on your
work?**

I have actually wondered whether I have gained or lost as a
woman, and sometimes I'm not very sure. Good things happen to
you because you are a woman and bad things happen to you
because you are a woman. I don't regret it. But I also know that I
have been sacrificed as a woman. If a man had been endowed as
I have been, he would probably have been able to accomplish
much more, because the opportunities would not be so controlled.
But I also know that I've been lucky, because I have gone through
many stages in my life—some of them have been successful and
some not. I think that many women, especially in Kenya, relate
to my story because they can almost read something in it that
reminds them of their own story. I know a lot of women also get
encouraged by the assistance of a vision and an aspiration, and
[the fact] that you're not putting a limit to yourself, that you're
almost taking literally the saying, "the sky is the limit."

**WW: Do you see yourself as a role model for women in
Kenya and beyond?**

Sometimes I've had difficult times and I think having those difficult times and overcoming them for the women is very important—that you don't have to be down and under. You can get

back up. I think that's what a lot of women relate to. I also think that's what men relate to now, because they figure, well, the story stopped being the story of a woman who is belligerent or a woman who is resisting being put in a certain place. You get out of there and they almost cannot help but admire the process. I think that is why now we have a public that is very receptive, whether it is men or women. That's very, very wonderful for women, because it's very encouraging.

I think a lot of women, especially women I was interacting with in the environmental movement, were very encouraged by the fact that I won an election. Maybe it would have been different if I had been nominated. They would probably have said, "Oh, some man somewhere decided to give her a position." So I am quite thrilled about it. I think I represent a different kind of woman, from where I come from and from the struggles I've had. I represent an ordinary woman—it's very different from coming into a position because of your inheritance. But me, I'm coming from any Dick and Harry; I'm a Dick and Harry of a woman.

WW: What's next? Do you see running for president one day?

Well, that is far-fetched right now. What I'm interested in is to see that I can make an impact in the government since I'm there, to see if I can really make a difference. It's also very important for me to perform at my constituency level. Then in five years I can say, "I'm glad I was there. I made a difference." If I come back the next time [to the government] it would be very good to be able to use the experience I will have gained during this first term. What the future brings, I really don't know. There are a lot of very young and very vibrant young men and women coming up; by the end of the second term I'll probably be feeling like I'm too tired.

WW: Do you think former President Moi is saying, "I can't believe that troublesome women got in there"?
I don't think so because he knew that the changes were very much part of the changes that we had dreamt about. People who were in the Moi government who are still in [government] positions are probably confused—they probably don't believe I can sit still and not be shouting at them. At the same time, I marvel at the fact that they are not in the government and we are now inside. I'm sure they sit there and wonder what the hell happened!

WW: With everything you've done you don't say, "I am going to do this." It's always "we." That's refreshing.
Once you work in civil society you know. I'm very conscious of the fact that you can't do it alone. It's teamwork. When you do it alone you run the risk that when you are no longer there nobody else will do it.

MARTIN ROWE, EDITOR
THE WAY OF COMPASSION
Vegetarianism, Environmentalism, Animal Advocacy, and Social Justice
"This eloquent, forceful body of writings . . . forges vital links between vegetarianism, environmentalism and animal rights and the quest for social justice."
—Publishers Weekly

RICHARD H. SCHWARTZ PHD
JUDAISM AND GLOBAL SURVIVAL
New Lantern Edition
"This book is not just for Jews. People of all faiths who want to know how the Hebrew Scriptures relate to the crucial issues of our times will find it invaluable. It can be common ground for those of us who want the kind of dialogue that will create the world that ought to be."
—Tony Campolo,
Professor Emeritus of Sociology, Eastern College